Well-Tuned Women

Growing Strong Through Voicework

Frankie Armstrong & Jenny Pearson, editors

First published by The Women's Press Ltd, 2000
A member of the Namara Group
34 Great Sutton Street, London EC1V OLQ
www.the-womens-press.com

Reprinted 2001

British Library Cataloguing-in-Publication Data
A catalogue record for this book is available from the British Library.

ISBN 0 7043 4649 4

Typeset in Trump Mediaeval 10pt/14pt by FiSH Books, London
Printed and bound in Great Britain by CPD (Wales) Ltd, Ebbw Vale

Acknowledgements

From Frankie

I would like to thank all those people, too numerous to name, who have been a source of encouragement, support and help over 43 years in my world of Voice, especially the participants and students in my Voice Workshops, from whom I have learnt so much.

From Frankie and Jenny

Our thanks to all the contributors to this book, who not only responded with great enthusiasm to the idea of it, but followed through with their highly original chapters and patient co-operation in the editorial process.

And our thanks to Charlotte Cole and The Women's Press, whose idea the whole thing was.

Contents

Preface

Historically, women's voices have been subject to social constraints and conditioning over the centuries and this heritage is still very much with us. When the natural voice is set free from these inhibitions, when we find ourselves giving full vocal expression to who we are and what we feel, this changes the way we experience ourselves in the world. We feel heard. We feel and become more confident, more effective. Hence our title *Well-Tuned Women* and the subtitle *Growing Strong Through Voice Work*.

The conception of this book was a collective one. The Women's Press approached us with a request for a book on the therapeutic aspect of voice work for women. Sitting in the kitchen of Jenny's house, we simultaneously came up with the idea of broadening the proposal to show how, by working with their voices, women can open the way to greater expressivity, creativity and a sense of freedom and effectiveness. So we suggested a book with contributions from a number of writers in a wide variety of social and professional settings, who would be able to demonstrate this general principle out of their work and experience. Thus the original meaning of 'therapeutic' was broadened to include the widest range of applications. We invited contributions on the history of the 'silencing' of women (Joan Mills); on the importance of the voice in women's response to physical threats (Annie Neligan on self-defence); and on the way vocalising can help our internal processes, including dealing with illness and disability (Frankie Armstrong, with testimonies from several women). There are also contributions about the surprising effects of voice work in psychiatric hospitals and war zones (Cicely Berry and Julie McNamara); in therapists' consulting rooms (Olivea Dewhurst-Maddock and Michele George); in the acting studio, business and politics (Patsy Rodenburg); in the community (Jenny Goodman); and in the vocally demanding work of teachers (Roz Comins). We asked for a chapter on an underlying issue for women: finding and recognising what is our fundamental voice (Kristin Linklater) and chapters on the experience of different ethnic groups, the power of their storytelling and song traditions (Nóirín Ní Riain, Ysaye Barnwell and Vayu Naidu) and the reawakening of the storyteller's voice in Britain (Jenny Pearson). There was some anxiety that with 15 contributors we might encounter a lot of repetition and overlap, necessitating some heavy pruning at the editorial stage. To our delight and astonishment, not one editorial decision had to be made on this account. What a tribute to the endless variety, richness, power, vulnerability and beauty of the tunes, tones and resonances of our voices!

The one consistent overlap is in the way the different contributions reflect the overall theme: how working with the voice involves a central area of our being, an area in which many women have felt themselves 'silenced' and how, in being helped to find our natural voice, we simultaneously experience a finding of ourselves and our expressivity. Our heartfelt thanks to our extraordinary contributors for taking time out from very busy lives to explore this issue with us, for following through with their completed chapters in spite of the hurdles life put in the way of some, and for their patience with the editorial process. Our thanks, also, to The Women's Press for setting in motion a project which has turned out to be so richly rewarding.

Frankie Armstrong and Jenny Pearson

A Vocal Album
Snapshots from Vocal History

Joan Mills

I first discovered the true power of the voice when I was
five years old. I see this moment as a photograph in an
imaginary archive: it is a winter's evening inside a village
church. Clearly it must be Christmas because the church
is decorated with holly, ivy, green branches with red
berries and is lit only by candlelight. Near the altar is a
crib and around it a group of children dressed as the figures
from the Nativity. Some are dressed in national costumes.
They are the Children of the World come to visit the Baby
Jesus. A small girl near the front is wearing the costume
which would then be called 'Eskimo'. It is not exactly an
authentic Inuit outfit, but the nearest her mother could
manage. She has on a thick sweater, a waistcoat and stout
corduroy trousers tucked into wellington boots, but most
important of all the wonderful hat her mother fashioned
from the bottom of an old possum coat. The ruff of long,
soft fur surrounds the child's small face and she is sure she
looks just like the drawing in her book about children
from other lands. At the moment my 'photograph' is
taken, she is singing the final verse of the carol *In the
Bleak Midwinter*:

> ...But what I can, I give him –
> Give my heart.

The child's voice rises bright and clear in the sweet
acoustic of the small church and if you were there you
would hear the congregation, all 300 or so, hold their

breath until the last notes die away. The silence that follows is not lost on the little girl. In that moment she relishes the power of being heard, of realising that she has the listeners in the palm of her hand – fellow children and, even more important, adults, who after all are inclined to say (it is 1953), 'children should be seen and not heard' . Of course I am rewriting history. All of this did happen, but any realisation was, at the time, an unconscious one. Only later in life did I recall that moment and connect it with a sense of empowerment through the voice.

There are other snapshots in this vocal album which I will return to later, but for the moment there is just one I would show you: I am 19, at university studying Drama, and auditioning for a role in one of the department's productions. I am very nervous. It is my first audition in the Drama department. The character is an exciting, bold woman, and with an energy and vocal quality I hope suits her I begin to read the speech:

'Four to one! How. . . ' That's as far as I get because I am interrupted.

'What? Four to what?' It is the director. He is one of the lecturers in the department. They are all pretty approachable but I am in awe of them all, and in this moment terrified by the question, which I don't understand, and his sharp tone of voice.

'Four to one,' I say, rather more quietly than I had begun.

'To what?' he demands.

'One,' I whisper.

'One.' He pronounces it slowly, rhyming it with gun.

'Not one,' he continues, rhyming it with on.

The tone in retrospect is not unkind; it is slightly amused. I am scarlet with embarrassment as his careful pronunciation of one word makes mockery of my odd mixture of Yorkshire and Shropshire. It is patently clear that the character of Donna Elvira (in Max Frisch's play *Don Juan and His Love of Geometry*) would never speak in such a voice. I stumble on through the rest of the speech, without heart, lamely attempting to clean up the appalling accent which has suddenly become obvious to me. I am not cast in the play but I am asked to be the assistant director. Directors, it seems, do not have to speak 'received pronunciation'. In the long run it turns out to be quite useful. I give up on performing until I manage to regain some confidence and consequently gather two years of technical and production skills invaluable to my future career as a theatre director.

I see these two snapshots from my vocal history reflected every day in the stories told in my voice workshops and classes. I often begin my workshops with a series of questions, the purpose of which is to allow the participants an opportunity to share their vocal fears quickly and relatively painlessly. I ask the participants if they remember their voices being the subject of a derogatory remark; even if it was when they were very small; even if they no longer believe what was said. If we explore these memories, the comments are the usual petty cruelties: 'who is the groaner in the second row?'; 'just mouth the words please'; 'that's not how a young lady should talk'; remarks about accent or dialect; unthinking jokes about the pitch or tone of the voice.

Yet there are also other recollections, a chance to savour moments of vocal confidence. I ask if the participants remember anyone remarking on the quality of their voices more positively (again no matter how long ago it may have been): perhaps to say how well they read or spoke or sang. Just as I appear in my two, contrasting 'snapshots', there will be many people who recall both experiences: they have felt the delight of drawing praise from the listener as well as the shame of criticism, sneers and derision.

Alfred Wolfsohn, vocal therapist and pioneer of techniques that allow the participant to explore the rich interaction of psyche and soma, resulting in the true and often extended range of the individual's voice, believed that if the voice is not given full expression then the whole person suffers. In effect, a suppressed voice causes the body and mind to sicken. Our voices are indeed ourselves. The voice is, in Wolfsohn's much quoted words, 'the muscle of the soul'. Our histories, whether men or women, are filled with times when to speak or to sing freely could mean ostracism, derision or even death. Survival depended on self-censorship, being extremely careful about the manner of speech or the mode of singing or, to be really safe – keeping silent.

When I analyse in detail what might restrain the evolution of the natural, free voice of anyone I work with, I look first to what might affect the body and breathing (and therefore, in turn, the power and quality of the voice): posture; clothing; movement; co-ordination; age; previous training; occupation; physical habits; and so on. Second I consider what other factors might be at play, particularly in the psyche, for instance: expectations of culture, gender, religion and class; family needs and hopes; regional differences; educational experiences; emotional and psychological development. Finally I must take into account the general context in which the person lives: the effect of the larger movements of the time, political ideology; fashion not only in clothing but in, for example, furniture; mode of speech and ideas; philosophy and music; technological developments; catastrophe, disease and war. Any and all of these factors might influence the speaking and singing voice.

I have grown up in a time when women have made enormous progress in the quest for equality and freedom, a time in which our voices have become recognised and as the twentieth century progressed – even celebrated. Yet I can recall many moments in my life when I felt silenced or censored, my voice seemed too small for my feelings, or too thin for the song, and I realise that the journey to free and explore my whole voice, both physically and psychologically, has been a long one; at times a real struggle as well as a pleasure. If this is true for me, born after the two World Wars which so radically changed women's status in Britain, how did the women of the past fare? What echoes can we perceive of their voices? I should say I am mainly limiting my view of the subject to my own cultural perspective. The sources I have used are Western, mostly European and North American. Views from other cultures are evident elsewhere in this book.

Is the history of these European and American women's voices to be read as a simple upward curve, a graph of gradual improvement in terms of both the right to speak and sing and the quality of vocal expression? Does it follow that as women's rights improved so did their voices? My own experiences as a voice practitioner in the context of psychological understandings of the late nineteenth and twentieth centuries suggest that 'our voices' encompasses not only *how* we speak but what and when, and that the ability to be heard, to be truly expressive, is deeply interwoven with possessing the right to speak, the freedom to enjoy communication. It follows that the evolution of the voices of women-past reflects as complex a pattern of development as the history of womankind itself. Traces of these voices are, however, not easy to find. In order to conjure up the voices of these women, from times before the invention of recorded sound, I need to become a 'voice detective', searching among past writings for small clues, or maybe a 'vocal archaeologist', sifting shards and fragments from another century for sounds. As Kate Emil-Behnke wrote in her book *Singers' Difficulties* in 1926:

The composer leaves his music, the painter his pictures, the sculptor his statues, the poet his verse, and therefore any accounts that are extant as to their methods will have great value to the student, taken in conjunction with their works. But the art of the singer and actor leaves nothing tangible behind; what they did, and how they accomplished it, is purely hearsay.

This is not true just of performers but of all speaking and singing. For most of our history the sound of the human voice is available to us only as writings about distant voices. History can tell us some of the conditions in which women lived, and even occasionally when and how they spoke, sang, told stories, performed – but still much can be known only by inference. It would be all too easy to imagine a simple scenario of gradual development – that as time has passed and women have made gains in the struggle for equal rights in education, work and the home, so they have felt more and more confident to let their voices be heard. Or to develop a theory that the voice of the modern woman is richer and fuller in tone because of greater freedom and self-determination in life generally. This view does not take into account the ups and downs of woman's status and is in danger of undervaluing the extraordinary achievements of our ancestors, women whose expressive, articulate voices spoke out and sang out against all odds and despite physical and cultural disadvantage.

In terms of physiology, however, we do know that improved health as a result of better diet, access to physical exercise and better medical care has resulted in women becoming taller, heavier and stronger in recent generations. These changes in the body may well affect the quality of sound and maybe the basic pitch of the voice, yet we should not forget that the majority of women, those of the poorer classes, at least until the industrial revolution, worked on the land, or the shore, in fresh air, developing strong muscles, calling and singing, talking with a freedom their upper class contemporaries might have been shocked to hear. Similarly, it is easy to assume that late twentieth century clothing is much less restrictive than that which our mothers and grandmothers wore, but anyone who has worn winkle-pickers with six-inch heels, tight, short skirts, uplift bras, power-dressing shoulder pads or ultra-slim-fit jeans (though hopefully not all at once), will know this to be a myth. Contemporary fashions can all too often be responsible for disturbed, unbalanced posture, restrained upper chest breathing, rigid abdominal muscles and all the vocal weaknesses that result.

The nineteenth century, however, was *the* time for hyperventilation and breathing difficulties caused by clothing. The boned corset created deformed rib cages and displacement of internal organs in millions of women. The only kind of breathing the Victorian well-dressed woman of the middle and upper class could manage was upper clavicle and any strong emotion or exertion brought on a fainting attack as a result. As to the effect on the voice, an increasing number of singing and elocution teachers in the last decades of the nineteenth century and early twentieth century were well aware of the problems corseting and poor breathing caused. Kate Emil-Behnke and her father were among the first voice practitioners to 'study the movements of breathing in relation to voice-use by means of X-rays'. From their studies they were able to point to the importance of 'avoiding any constriction of clothing which might prevent the descent of the diaphragm and thereby cause pressure on the heart in strong exercise'. Vocal problems were bound to result from such constriction.

> The regulation and control of expiration are so difficult in upper chest breathing as to be well nigh impossible; and the effort entailed is so great as to cause gasping, wrong attack of tone, congestion of the vessels of the throat, muscular fatigue, faulty intonation, unevenness, tremolo, and inability to sustain a long phrase.
>
> *Singers' Difficulties*, Kate Emil-Behnke, 1926

The speaking voice which resulted would have been the breathy, thin, high and unresonant rather childlike voices we associate with some of Dickens' female characters, but which might have been considered a sweet, pleasing and feminine tone by many at the time. By the end of the twentieth century, books of advice on health and beauty for young women were extolling the virtues of exercise, deep breathing and the avoidance of all tight-lacing. It is no coincidence that this was also precisely the time women were beginning their real fight for independence: improvement in legal status, and a voice in politics.

As I mentioned earlier, it is not only the physical conditions we must examine to get an idea of the 'vocal climate' for women. The temper of the times, the expectations and pressures exerted by society are vital. From the earliest historical accounts we can see that the right of women to speak *at all* has been denied time after time and in many cultures. Discussing Roman women, Charles Seltman, in *Women in Antiquity*, tells us:

> ...in Rome her life was one of legal incapacity which amounted to enslavement, while her status was described as 'imbecilitas', whence our word. Naturally she had no say in public affairs or office, and was ranked as a permanent minor.

Silence was essential if these dangerous, 'imbecilic', childlike creatures no wiser than animals were to be kept under control.

If women were never allowed to speak publicly it seems likely that their abilities in the area of debate, public speaking or oratory would be very poor. But of course oppression breeds revolt and the human need for self-expression is strong even in extremely difficult circumstances. In 195BC, when crowds of women thronged the Capitol to oppose the Oppian Law which was so oppressive to women, the consul Marcus Porcius Cato addressed the protesters:

> What do you mean by coming out in public in this unheard of fashion and calling out to other women's husbands? Could you not have raised all these matters at home and with your own husbands?...Woman is a violent and uncontrolled animal, and it is useless to let go the reins and then expect her not to kick over the traces.
>
> *The History of Rome*, Livy

It is easy to generalise and assume that men were always the oppressors. This is certainly not the case and it is important to recognise that just as in our own times there are opposing views about the abilities of women and whether their voices should be heard in political, spiritual and cultural life, so the same debates raged in the Greek and Roman eras. Then, as now, not all men were intent on silencing the female voice. In the early first century AD the orator and lawyer Quintilian envisaged education as including girls for he could see the benefits to children of having both parents well educated and saw that women had already made achievements in the art of oratory:

> Cornelia, the mother of Gracchi [whose very learned writing in her letters has come down to posterity], contributed greatly to their eloquence; the daughter of Laelius is said to have exhibited her father's elegance in conversation; and the oration of the daughter of Quintus Hortensius, delivered before the Triumviri [pleading for a partial remission of the tax laid on matrons], is read not merely as an honour to her sex.
>
> *Institutes of Oratory*, Quintilian

Women were also admired for extending the boundaries

of the right to speak and for developing the performing arts and the expressive voice:

> Well educated in Greek and Latin literature, [Sempronia] had greater skill in lyre-playing and dancing than there is any need for a respectable woman to acquire...She could write poetry, crack a joke, and converse at will with decorum, tender feeling or wantonness; she was in fact a woman of ready wit and considerable charm.
>
> *The Conspiracy of Catiline*, Sallust

Sallust's implication (despite his obvious admiration of Sempronia), that a woman accomplished as a singer, musician or dancer was likely to be a prostitute, can be found throughout history. Women, like children, should be seen and not heard. It is somehow 'unwomanly' to be so entertaining. Performance, public speaking, witty, educated conversation are all considered within the male domain and yet clearly very attractive and effective when carried out by a woman. The confusion may be relieved by separating out such women, by removing them from the same category as wives and mothers, by seeing them as women who do not have to be respected – whores. This view of female performers, whose powerful voices and bodies were so attractive and threatening, persisted throughout the centuries and it is only relatively recently that actresses and singers have been seen as respectable women.

Even being a practising Christian would not save a woman from such accusations if she dared to use her voice to communicate her religious beliefs herself, rather than through a man.

> Let your women keep silence in the churches for it is not permitted unto them to speak; but they are

commanded to be under obedience...And if they will learn anything, let them ask their husbands at home: for it is a shame for a woman to speak in church.

Timothy 2:12–15

And hence, later, the criticisms launched at Quakers and other women who dared to claim the right to be 'filled with the word of God and thus be able to preach and teach'. How shocking it was

...to see bold impudent housewives, without all womanly modesty, to take upon them (in the natural volubility of their tongues, and quick wits or strong memories only) to prate [not preach or prophesy] after a narrative or discoursing manner, an hour or more, and that most directly contrary to the Apostle's inhibition...

The Schismatick Sifted, John Vicars, 1646

Clearly there is to be no simple graph of improved conditions for the development of women's voices as time passes. Though any kind of view of these 'vociferous' women is certainly an advance on the attitudes revealed at the sixth century debate in Macon, held in all seriousness to discuss whether women actually had souls or not. (Had the British apostolic prelates of Glastonbury not held the day there would have been little chance of the women of the next few centuries being heard at all.) This climate of vocal oppression can be traced throughout the centuries. Silencing can be ensured through the law or other institutions like the church which make it impossible for women to speak in public, to perform or even to argue with their husbands. It can be institutionalised by excluding women from educational opportunities or proscribing their behaviour. Manuals of conduct, books of advice give us some idea of how women were expected to be and to sound. Even the feminist writer Christine de Pisan has a warning for single women, but considering the likely punishments of the time if one strayed beyond accepted behaviour, perhaps she was trying to do them a favour:

> Let them [young girls and widows]...have a sedate expression and be sober of speech, bearing and smile.
>
> Christine de Pisan, c.1420

By the early sixteenth century, Baldassare Castiglioni's book on courtly behaviour, *Il Cortegiano*, is suggesting another role for ladies (of aristocratic and courtly circles at least), and his ideas were to be extremely influential, the book being reprinted many times in all major European languages. For the first time it is suggested that women other than nuns and prostitutes had a role to play outside family and household. In particular Castiglioni suggested a woman might

> ...entertain graciously every kind of man with agreeable and comely conversation suited to the time and place and to the station of the person with whom she speaks...the Court lady must have not only the good judgement to recognise the kind of person with whom she is speaking, but must have knowledge of many things in order to entertain that person graciously...her discourse will be fluent and most prudent, virtuous and pleasant.

He has a high opinion of women's abilities in general and asks:

> Do you not remember reading of many women who were learned in philosophy? Others who excelled in poetry? Others who prosecuted, accused and defended before judges with great eloquence?

Becoming a nun had been a course of action taken by many independent minded women throughout the centuries in order to avoid unwanted marriages and family demands, or to be free to study and be creative. Hildegard of Bingen, the twelfth century writer, composer and visionary, perhaps first springs to mind, but even as early as the tenth century, Hrotsvitha, Benedictine nun of Gandershaim, became the first female playwright, her plays being enacted by the nuns and maybe Hrotsvitha herself. Yet still women upon a stage were regarded as shameless and when a French theatre company came to London during King Charles I's reign an eye witness proclaimed:

> Glad am I to say that they were hissed, hooted and pippin-pelted from the stage, so that I do not think they will soon be ready to try the same again.

Despite the fact that several royal women had taken part in masques both singing and performing, and that a certain Mrs Coleman had even broken the laws preventing women from acting by playing a role in *The Siege of Rhodes*, albeit in a private residence, women did not appear in professional plays in this country until 1660, when King Charles II granted a Royal Charter to Thomas Killigrew and Sir William Davenant to create a company of players and the Drury Lane Theatre. The charter contained the vital and revolutionary phrase:

> ...And wee doe likewise permit and give leave that all the woemen's part to be acted in either of the said two companies for the time to come may be performed by woemen...

At the stroke of the royal pen women were admitted to a profession where they would be able to use their voices with freedom and expressivity so often denied them in everyday life. Beginning then with Margaret Hughes, innumerable actresses captured the hearts of the theatre-going public. Among them were those who became the most famous women of the seventeenth, eighteenth and nineteenth centuries: Nell Gwynne, Nance (Anne) Oldfield, Peg Woffington, Marie (later Lady) Bancroft, Sarah Siddons and Ellen Terry. They were friends with lords and dukes, dined at the great houses, and were courted by kings. They had come a long way since the days when to perform was to be declared a prostitute or told to keep silent. Of Sarah Siddons Tate Wilkinson said: 'If you ask me what is a Queen? I should say, Mrs Siddons.'

> Lord Erskine, a notable orator, said that Siddons' performances were a school for oratory, and that he studied her cadences and intonations [which] enabled him to improve his own eloquence...Her voice, always perfectly controlled, was in the main plaintive, often melancholy – but it could ring like a clarion call or be sonorous as an organ diapason. She could utter a shriek at moments of doom which pierced the very soul of her audience.
>
> *Ladies First*, W Mcqueen-Pope, 1952

Yet while these women were gaining ground, and displaying the full range of the expressive capabilities of the voice with such intelligence and originality, for many the continuous insistence on their not taxing their poor little brains with anything other than discussion of domestic matters or pretty patter continued. What underlies this insistence on avoidance of serious talk and the encouraging of simpering, 'light' conversation is a recurring belief in the female weakness of mind. There are endless examples throughout the centuries but this one from the early twentieth century is typical. P Mobius, a German scientist, in *Concerning the Physiological Intellectual Feebleness of Women* (1907) wrote:

> Important parts of the brain necessary for spiritual life, the frontal convolutions and the temporal lobes, are less well developed in women and this difference is inborn...If the feminine abilities were developed to the same degree as those of the male, her maternal organs would suffer and we should have before us a repulsive and useless hybrid.

Thus relieved of all worldly responsibilities and serious thought or talk, the woman's place was in the home and indeed, according to Coventry Patmore, her role was to be that of 'The Angel in the House', while Tennyson proclaimed her: 'No angel, but a dearer being, all dipt in angel instincts, breathing Paradise...' Mrs Sarah Stickney Ellis, a nineteenth century novelist, made the arrangement very clear:

> It is the privilege of a married woman to be able to show by the most delicate attentions how much she feels her husband's superiority to herself...by respectful deference to his opinion, and a willingly imposed silence when he speaks.

When women did speak it was understood that the tone would be sweet and the language not too wild or extravagant:

> 'Did you notice Mrs B—'s new shawl, last Sabbath?' Inquired one young lady of another; 'wasn't it splendid?'
> 'Yes; it was perfectly magnificent!'
> 'What a horrid bonnet Miss M— had on, at church!' Exclaimed another young woman...
> This style of conversation is not feminine. It becomes the bar-room better than the parlour. 'Pretty' is a better

word than 'splendid', 'homely' than 'horrid', and 'beautiful' than 'magnificent', in the connection in which they are used. Girls should also avoid swearing in conversation...some young ladies employ a class of epithets which well deserve the appellation of feminine profanity. Such are the words gracious, mercy, vow, goodness and others like them. If not so wicked, they are nearly as unbecoming to women as the vile oaths of the bar-room are to men...The use of the tongue is a matter of no trivial account. Not merely as an item of manners, but as a moral consideration, it is of great moment.

The True Woman, William M Thayer, 1896

In a stifling cultural climate which attempted to exclude her from education, and which demanded such vocal restraint, learning to speak publicly, to deliver a lecture for example must have been a real difficulty. Annie Besant, who made a career eventually as a public orator, activist and pamphleteer, writes of the first lecture she ever gave – delivered to no one in an empty church:

I thought I would like to try how it felt to speak from the pulpit. Some vague fancies were stirring in me that I could speak if I had the chance; very vague they were, for the notion that I might ever speak on the platform had never dawned on me; only the longing to find outlet in words was in me; the feeling that I had something to say, and the yearning to say it...I shall never forget the feeling of power and of delight which came upon me as my voice rolled down the aisles, and the passion in me broke into balanced sentences, and never paused for rhythmical expression, while I felt all I wanted was to see the church full of upturned faces, instead of the emptiness of the silent pews. And as though in a dream the solitude became peopled and I saw the listening faces and the eager eyes, and as the sentences came unbidden from my lips, and my own tones echoed back to me from the pillars of the ancient church, I knew of a verity that the gift of speech was mine.

Autobiographical Sketches, Annie Besant, 1885

There were means of vocal expression, however, that had been in the ordinary woman's keeping for centuries, which were not public and were handed down through oral transmission, practised in private. These included the telling of stories, singing of lullabies, performance of newly created, popular songs as well as traditional songs, often associated with particular seasonal or social rituals and events. The industrial revolution, the coming of radio and later television meant the loss of many such songs and the traditions which went with them. Some of these have been rediscovered in the late twentieth century, however, such as singing to the dying for example. In Marjorie Kennedy-Fraser's collection, *Songs of the Hebrides* (1909), there are several such 'Death Croons', originally sung over the dying to ease their passage to death, by women who were very often also the midwives and had equally helped many into life. During the past 20 years a number of organisations, such as The Chalice of Repose led by Therese Schroeder-Sheker, have revived these ancient skills and helped the terminally ill or old let go of life by similar means.

At the turn of the century women were fighting hard for the right to speak and be heard, breaking the silence imposed by Victorian society to speak publicly in meetings which were often outdoors, and in situations which put them at great personal risk. The vocal energy needed to be heard over a crowd of men (and women) determined to shout the speakers down must have quickly developed the lung power and articulation ability of the 'feeble' minded and bodied women who dared to insist on communicating their ideas and making their feelings clear. Nevertheless it took courage to continue in the face of such determination to silence them. When Josephine Butler sought to hold a meeting against state regulation of prostitution she had to go all over the town 'before we found anyone bold enough to grant us a place to meet in'. When they eventually found a hay loft large enough, they discovered once the large crowd came in, 'the floor strewn with cayenne pepper in order to make it impossible for us to speak'.

After two world wars, during which women took on almost any work that would have been done previously by men, when their physical courage as medical staff, drivers, labourers, and members of the armed forces was without question, it seemed as though they had won the right to speak and be heard. Yet in spite of having won the vote, improvements in legal and marital status and the possibility of education and work, in 1948 women were still being advised in their magazines to 'take an interest in his hobbies' in order to hold a conversation that would engage *him*.

Glorify Yourself, was a magazine series that showed ordinary women the secrets of the movie studio stars she so admired on the big screen, secrets which once mastered would ensure her success in attracting the right man. One issue reveals speech and conversation techniques that are crucial for her to learn. The advice, from the stars' personal coaches Eleanor King or Terry Hunt, is to become a lively and skilled conversationalist because 'nothing so enhances a person's charm as does a colourful, yet gracious manner of speech' and 'good conversation can make you more popular'. In order to improve her speech technique the woman of 1948 was advised to practise a variety of vocal exercises in front of a mirror and repeat words which might prove tricky. Why tricky? Because she had to be sure when pronouncing such words as 'vacant', 'vanity' or 'friend' not to let the front teeth touch the lower lip and thus transfer lipstick (an essential in the 1940s) to the teeth. The result is a slightly pouting mode of speech which can be observed in films of the era!

Equally she was to be sure to avoid pulling the mouth out of shape when speaking a variety of consonants and vowels, especially 'o':

> Here I should like to point out the outstanding sounds which mar the appearance of your lips. They are the sounds of 'oo', 'ee', 'p', 'h', 'w', 'g' and 'y'...Supposing that each time a woman says the letter 'o' she drops her jaw an inch, at the same time rounding her lips into a perfect circle...Since 'o' is such a common letter in our alphabet, she says it dozens of times daily. Isn't it reasonable that this one speech habit deepens the hollows in her cheeks and the wrinkles around her lips? With just a little practice you can learn to pronounce them correctly and STILL KEEP THE LOWER PART OF YOUR FACE ATTRACTIVE [original caps!].

According to Ms King, preserving your beauty is all a matter of 'good speech habits'. Another section deals with how to hold the 'short' or 'long' conversation, again with the emphasis on the woman keeping the conversation going by engaging his interest and staying very positive. She is given warnings and tips: 'Don't be loud in public', 'Don't complain, especially in male company', 'DO pause frequently when speaking. Men particularly dislike non-stop feminine voices...Don't interrupt...' The whole aim of this facility with language and vocal tone is to attract a husband or once married to be a credit to him. That gaining such vocal confidence may help you to get and keep a job is mentioned, but it is also clear that the workplace is merely a hunting ground for the right man, and will be of no use once you have found a suitable husband. The physical instructions which accompanied these voice notes were detailed down to every gesture and included footwork worthy of any member of the Royal Ballet, for example 'How to turn in a doorway' and the 'Social Pivot'. Posture was considered particularly important and required the reader to learn to walk in high heeled shoes along a chalk line, holding the abdominal muscles in and raising the chest.

As your buttock muscles tighten when you push your coccyx forward, do you notice that your abdominal muscles contract also? They do and your abdomen looks flatter.

I have met many women of around my age who still carry themselves with this kind of postural combination and cannot release the abdominal muscles or manage abdominal breathing exercises as a result. One woman in a workshop I was leading a few years ago eventually overcame this ingrained habit and, having embraced the deep relaxed breathing we were aiming for, announced that she had not let go of those muscles for over 30 years, her mother having trained her to always pull in the belly area to flatten it as much as possible in order to be attractive. Within the last decade, however, many of the young actors and theatre students I have trained have exactly the same habit, convinced that any relaxation of these abdominal muscles will disqualify them from achieving the current 'size-10-or-less' look.

Theatre and films of the 1950s and 60s that demonstrated these rules of voice and gesture were a huge influence on me. I was taken to the cinema every Friday evening with my family and also watched my father in amateur theatre performances whose style attempted to emulate the great actors of the 1930s and 1940s. The men in these plays and films were heroes and got to do and say bold and exciting things. The films we saw were mostly my father's choice. As a consequence I grew up on a diet of cowboys n' indians and war movies. Many of the women in the films seemed to have bold, defiant, free lives until they fell in love and submitted to the sweet embrace of a handsome hunk. I longed to sound and look like Doris Day in *Calamity Jane* but only while she was riding horses, singing on the stagecoach and toting a gun. When she became a little homemaker in the log cabin and moderated her voice, I lost interest. At the Wolverhampton Hippodrome I saw Janette Scott as Peter Pan, *really* flying through the air and speaking and calling out with the wild carelessness of a boy. Here is another snapshot for my vocal album – me aged nine leaping out of a tree whooping and calling Peter's 'Cock-a-doodle-doo' of triumph which so curdled the blood of Captain Hook. Later, in my teenage years, came television and the amazingly self-confident and physically superior Emma Peel in *The Avengers* became a new role model. This necessitates taking up judo and another vocal snap for the archive as I throw my partner and call out wonderfully mysterious Japanese words. I buy black stretch trousers and waistcoat and desperately attempt to develop Mrs Peel's cool but assured vocal delivery.

As for singing, the radio provided great role models like Peggy Lee with her terrific earthy 'Fever' sung by me in a great, deep voice aged about nine, or songs like 'Sixteen Tons' sung by Tennessee Ernie in an even deeper voice! Later, the sweet higher pitched sound of Joan Baez accorded exactly with what my voice had become after the seven years in church and school choirs and even though perhaps it was a bit too sweet, what I saw was a woman out there alone, centre stage, her voice raised in protest or singing the old ballads, stories of love and despair, struggle and triumph – what could be more of an inspiration for a 15-year-old with an acoustic guitar bought for her by an astute American aunt? So I searched out more of these old, mostly forgotten songs to take into folk club performances, which allowed me to once more sense that hush, that attention which nurtured my sense of self-esteem. Thus an awkward, incredibly shy teenager, for those moments on stage gained an articulate voice and felt the adults listening instead of insisting on silence.

The girls' high school I attended was averse to most talking, all shrieking or shouting, and was very hot on silence: in corridors, classes, the library, assembly. When and where were we to find a voice? When we talked it had to be in a 'ladylike way' and 'properly', that is making sure we did not leave off the h's or sound hard g's in singing or coat-hanger (like my friend Carol who was forever shamed in front of the class for her broad Shropshire). We even had to avoid reading too expressively – I was left out of the Christmas concert for doing that. Fortunately there were occasional English or Music teachers who made that space for us. God Bless Mrs Jackson, Miss Wareham and others. The songs I sang, the parts I played in school plays gave me room to explore my voice which the rest of life did not. The church choir, the school plays, the local amateur drama group were the havens within which my sense of self and voice grew while in everyday life I stumbled and mumbled or stayed as quiet as my nickname: Mouse.

My upbringing was a torment of fear: of doing or of saying the wrong thing; of unnamed sexual and worldly matters I knew I would meet and be ill-equipped to deal with. This was reflected in a gauche, anxious body, unbalanced, ungrounded, seemingly leg-less – all my energy being directed by well meaning educationalists away from the powerhouse of sexual organs and belly to the thinking area, the brain. My voice reflected this imbalance and, while sweet and clear, was that of a boy treble even when a young woman. The places I found in which to explore my voice, the teachers who encouraged, the theatre training all helped me to develop my right to speak as well as my actual voice. Life experience – falling in and out of love, discovering I was after all perfectly well equipped to deal with sex, and the perils and joys of working in theatre – did the rest, so that when, over the years, opportunities arose to train with voice and physical theatre practitioners from a variety of cultures, I was more than ready to embrace the outer limits of my voice and body and include them in what I feel to be my self.

In 1980 I joined the organisation later to become the Centre for Performance Research. It was then I began to research voice techniques from around the world in preparation for Project Voice, CPR's first voice gathering. In 1990 we began Giving Voice, a series of themed gatherings of international voice practitioners which celebrates and explores the human voice. At Giving Voice, as well as other voice meetings and conferences I have attended, I realise how many women there are among the outstanding teachers and performers. Of the 192 voice practitioners who have taught or performed at the CPR to date, 100 are women, while at the Royal Shakespeare Company's Voice '92 meeting which especially brought together voice coaches and teachers, 40 out of the 48 voice practitioners invited were women. Have women perhaps developed a particular ability to understand vocal fears and to encourage vocal development because of their collective history of vocal suppression? Whatever the reasons, as we enter the twenty-first century, women's voices are certainly as audible as women themselves are now visible.

During the late twentieth century, in Europe and North America at least, women have taken the opportunities afforded by improvements in their social, economic, political and cultural status to develop a voice, in both the sense of a right to speak or sing freely and the techniques to do so, with skill and expression. Women's voices have been heard in each of those contexts that were denied to all but the most fearless, privileged or gifted in previous centuries: in politics; in performance, both stage and screen; in classical and popular music; in the church, law and education. They have led the singing at Civil Rights marches and been raised against the siting of American missiles at Greenham. Solo, they have made us laugh in comedy clubs, and in chorus tickled the ear with the harmony of community choirs. They have coached and developed the voices of some of the most outstanding artists of the day and creatively developed vocal techniques often pioneered by their nineteenth and early twentieth century sisters.

So here is a final snapshot for my vocal archive: though this time I admit it is an invention. I am standing with a group of women somewhere in the open air on a clear and sunny day; their clothing is unusual in that it includes styles from the past two millennia and even before; we are singing together or are we perhaps, as women will sometimes, talking all at once? We have the look of those who have managed to survive any amount of negative comment: a determination to be heard. We look at the camera, straight into the lens, bodies released and straight, and our mouths are open wide. Can you hear us?

Bibliography

Emil-Behnke, Kate, *Singers' Difficulties*, Cassell & Co, London, 1926

Hays, HR, *The Dangerous Sex*, Methuen, London, 1966

Horowitz Murray, Janet, *Strong Minded Women*, Penguin, London, 1984

Mcqueen-Pope, W, *Ladies First: The Story of Woman's Conquest of the British Stage*, WH Allen, London, 1952

O'Faolain Julia and Martines, Lauro, *Not in God's Image*, Virago, London, 1979

Seltman, Charles, *Women in Antiquity*, Pan, London, 1956

Thayer, William, M, *The True Woman*, Hodder and
    Stoughton, London, 1896
Glorify Yourself: A Women's Journal, Psychology
    Publishing Co. Ltd, 1948–52

Overtones, Undertones and the Fundamental Pitch of the Female Voice

Kristin Linklater

> Patience is sottish and impatience does
> Become a dog that's mad.
> Cleopatra, *Antony and Cleopatra*

I have a book, published in 1903, entitled *Mary: The Perfect Woman*. In a chapter headed 'Qualifications for Married Life' there is a subheading, 'Desirable Traits of Character in a Woman', where we learn that:

> Women should be gentle – not weak, but gentle, and kind, and affectionate. Whatever a woman is, there should be a sweet, subduing and harmonizing influence of purity, and truth, and love, pervading and hallowing, from center to circumference, the entire circle in which she moves. If the men are savages we want her to be their civilizer. We want her to soften their manners, and to teach them all needful lessons of order, sobriety, and meekness, and patience, and goodness.

Warning against an addiction to pleasure and excitement the book admonishes:

> Woman's life is made up of little pleasures, of little tasks, of little cares, and little duties, but which, when added together, make a grand total of human happiness; she is not expected to do any arduous work; her province lies in gentleness, in cheerfulness, in contentment, in housewifery, in care and management

of her children, in sweetening her home. These are emphatically a heritage, her jewels, which help to make up her crown of glory.

It has taken the twentieth century to prove that these ideals of feminine perfection constitute a vast repression of the whole human being that is a woman. My quotation from Cleopatra, at the beginning of this examination of women's voices, highlights the dilemma women experience in the course of trying to figure out how to live in this world. Patiently putting up with the *status quo* is stupid, but if you get impatient and behave badly, people say you are crazy. Cleopatra is a woman 'Whom every thing becomes, to chide, to laugh/ To weep: how every passion fully strives/ To make itself in thee, fair and admired!' She may not be the ideal role model, but she is more interesting than The Perfect Woman: 'I saw her once' says Enobarbus, 'Hop forty paces through the public street/ And having lost her breath, she spoke, and panted,/ That she did make defect perfection,/ And breathless, power breathe forth'. One might say her pitch was fundamentally hers. Many of us still feel that we speak in a patient undertone or a strident overtone, but are not really in tune with ourselves or our society.

Society at large provides no sounding-board for the harmonics of women's voices; at best it absorbs the vibrations, muffling them in a cloak of indulgence, at worst it isolates and ridicules them. The sound of our own voices as women is as confusing as it is liberating because it is a sound which confuses the harmonics of our society.

Men live in a reliable 'sound-house'. Men hear their voices reverberating into and back from the community and the body politic, confirming the validity of their thoughts, words and emotions. 'I speak; I am heard; therefore I am' offers at least a skeletal sense of identity. If a culture could be thought to have vocal cords, those of our society would vibrate with male frequencies; the bass notes of the patriarchy provide a fundamental pitch or tone around which the frequencies of the female voice are heard as overtones and undertones. The cultural 'sound-house' is patriarchal.

If we could invoke a kind of archaeological sonogram to search out those places where in the past women's voices have resounded in ways that affirmed them in their identity, we would enter the 'sound-houses' of the nursery, the kitchen, the bedroom and, according to the women's station in life, perhaps the fields or the garden. A woman's voice and her sense of self were secure in crooning and babbling to the baby and in her storytelling to the older children. Her identity was clear in her duty to the dead, in ritual and regular mourning, keening and wailing. Her voice had authority in the kitchen and at mealtimes. The weaving and spinning worked well when she sang. She knew the cattle would come when she called and the hens would come running when she made *chook chook* noises and rattled the pail. She could advertise her stock of fresh violets or fresh herrings in a high, clear chant that would cut across the noise of crowded streets. Women preserved the bawdy stories, the raunchy tittle-tattle of the bedroom and shared among themselves the would-be secrets of the sexual proclivities and idiosyncrasies of men. They were domestic bards. Singing, storytelling, laughing, weeping and calling, they knew who they were within their sound-houses as they heard the sure vibrations of their presence reverberate in these accustomed surroundings. Their voices had a wide range: high for the calling and keening, low for the crooning.

But now we want to reverberate in the wide resonance chambers of the world. Paradoxically, as our resonating chambers have grown larger, our voices have tended to diminish in range. Women tend to be stuck in a high voice or a low voice or in two notes in the middle of their registers, with their identities similarly constricted. The natural wide range, from exuberance to cradling calm, has been unable to find a sound-house outside the domestic arena.

As we enter a new century we are in the middle of a discordant passage, straining towards an ideal chorus. Could there be a balance between the treble voice of the female psyche and the bass voice of the male psyche, with contralto and tenor tones making harmonies proportionate to the male/female proportions in the population of the world?

At this point we need to look for and consciously construct, with female vibrations, sound-houses that will re-sound the lives of women realistically. Most people think that the quality of their voice is genetically and anatomically predetermined, but nurture and culture are, in fact, the major determinants of vocal quality and vocal behaviour. The cultural rules women unconsciously obey are that their voices should be high and helpless or low and gentle. If women's voices are low and strong they break balls.

A high, light voice in a woman stereotypically signals a sexy helplessness. As one part of her semiotic apparatus this may be useful to a woman, but if her voice only knows the top few notes of her diapason they will prove to be more of a liability than an asset when she wants to express other aspects of her personality or even her emotional needs. When a high voice connects with a strong impulse based, for instance, in anger or fear, it becomes shrill, strident, screechy, piercing, nasal, penetrating, sharp, squeaky or brassy and generally unpleasant to the point of causing major distress in the hearers.

The deeper ranges of the voice connect with the self at a fundamental level of power and many women avoid the feeling and expression of power because they do not want to dominate. Power has a bad history. It is possible that if women's voices were free they could transform the reputation of power, from despotic to an articulation of powerful gentleness, powerful caring, powerful joy, powerful laughter and the powerful vulnerability that is the prerequisite for powerful compassion.

Is this The Perfect Woman in a new dress? No! It is utterly unrealistic to pretend that women are the natural progenitors and guardians of only positive emotions. We also need the so-called 'negative' emotions in order to develop the emotional muscle, resilience and stamina that make softer feelings safe. Centuries of gossip, storytelling and relationships have exercised women in emotions that include anger, grief and even hate as legitimate and manageable members of our emotional universe. When we are merely nice and polite we become emotionally flabby and our voices lose muscle tone. We do not need to repress our emotions but to allow each one its own democratic state, each with its own voice. The strong ones that have attack potential will protect the vulnerable ones that open the doors to the self. We become emotionally fit with well-exercised voices at our command. Taken together, these would create realistic sound-houses in the world.

The fact that women's voices are drowned out by the bass notes of men can be examined from emotional, historical, political, cultural, familial, mythological, psychological and sociological angles. For a particular historical perspective I am beholden to Nor Hall (*The Moon and the Virgin; Those Women*) for introducing me to Maud Gleason's *Making Men: Sophists and Self-Presentation in Ancient Rome* and Anne Carson's *Glass and God*. Nor Hall told the story of the fourth century teacher Labanius who taught men that they must cultivate their voices to uphold their superiority. Their testicles functioned as 'loom-weights' to the vocal cords, thus deepening the voice. If a man, leaving his house in the morning, met someone whose voice was 'unhung' – a woman, or a eunuch – he was advised to go back home and start the day again. In classical Greece the cries of women – shrieking, wailing, sobbing, shrill lament, loud laughter, screams of pain or pleasure and eruptions of raw emotions – were not encouraged within the bounds of the city or within earshot of men (Anne Carson). We can do nothing but marvel at these glimpses of historical/patriarchal prejudice and notice the evidence of its continuing presence.

Searching for a contemporary perspective that could signpost avenues of potential change in the vocal *status quo*, I am led by Carol Gilligan to listen to girls. Girls of 9, 10, 11 years old are often told: 'You're too noisy, too pushy, too bossy, too clever for your own good!' At these ages they often have big, strong voices with a wide, revealing range. They are emotionally intrepid. By the time they are adolescents they become prime subjects for studies in low self-esteem. Then they become women. Paying attention to the quality of girls' voices before their adolescent acculturation reveals that, between girlhood and womanhood, clarity and directness of expression are sacrificed in order not to compete with the patriarchal fundamental.

Carol Gilligan's *In A Different Voice*, published in 1982, was a major milestone in feminist literature. Gilligan says that when the voices of women enter the human conversation, the conversation will change profoundly and disturbingly. The 11-year-old Amy in her book solves moral problems from a completely different point of view to that of 11-year-old Jake. In Gilligan's subsequent work with the Harvard Project on Women's Psychology and Girls' Development, a picture emerged of young girls with a startling outspokenness and clarity of perception which lasted until the edge of adolescence. From the age of 12 or 13 girls began to retreat, to cover up, to 'go underground'. They grew more silent, veiling their perceptions in 'I don't know'.

About this we can surely do something. We can build new sound-houses that are tuned to the vibrations of girls and amplify the fundamental pitch of women's voices. Women are already powerfully positioned for acoustical revolution. They dominate the educational scene. The classroom is equal to the home in developmental influence. In kindergarten and elementary school most of the teachers are women. In high school women teachers still outnumber men; in higher education the proportion swings heavily to a male bias.

We accept the way we learn in school as normal. But is it normal to respect our brains more than our bodies and to split our minds from our hearts? The conditioning we receive in school and college through a disembodied mode of learning was developed initially to educate boys. Boys needed early conditioning to be able to separate from their homes and parents and prepare themselves for a life out in the world – trading, fighting, travelling, governing. They had to forget the needs of the heart and lose their soft sensibilities if they were to succeed. Intellect and reason had to be cut off from emotion and sensuality. This remains a *de facto* philosophy of our present educational systems.

Boys also suffer from this dis-education, but they have the advantage of a schooling made by men that trains them to succeed in a world made by men. Girls are torn out of their natures and forced into an educational mould that does not recognise any of their contours. From the age of 13 they are aliens, with no one speaking their psychic language. And they adapt, at incalculable cost, to the very society that dictates these measures for survival.

In kindergarten and through the lower grades of elementary school we are taught to co-operate and play together, sing songs together, build things, act things out, paint and share. Our teachers comfort us when we cry, they make sure that we eat our morning snack and that we take our naps. It is a holistic learning imbued with the arts.

By the time we are in high school the arts are taken less seriously than goal-oriented subjects which enable us to compete in the market-place. Our teachers no longer pay attention to whether we are feeling all right or are eating properly. We learn not to cry, to disguise our feelings, to hide our secrets so that we can fool the competition. We draw ourselves up into our brains, out of our bodies. It is clearly stupid to care or share or sing or paint or act. Education is delivered to the brain, not to the whole person.

The higher we go in 'higher education', the fewer women are found in the classrooms and lecture halls. The educational class system delivers a clear message: women teach in the lower classes and what they teach is of lower value than the aristocratic pedagogy of pure intellect, reason and logic found at the top of the educational ladder. The implied message is that emotions are counter-productive, sharing is dangerous, togetherness is sentimental and the arts are irrational: are all these 'women's things' and without value.

The challenge now, as I see it, is for women who teach in high schools and higher education to be true to their own perceptions and voices and to listen to the voices of the girls in their classrooms, nurturing them as they are and not as the world dictates. Women are traditionally brought up to be nice and polite, particularly to men. At the same time those of us with a 'nice' upbringing are also encouraged to tell the truth. What an impossible situation! We women must surely acknowledge that we have been rigorously trained in the art of prevarication. We have been raised to dodge the issue, to be vocally and verbally devious for the sake of peace and quiet in our society. We become liars. And it is women who teach us how.

Can women who teach girls break this pattern and encourage the girls to express themselves and their perceptions of the world, while at the same time protecting them from the dangers they will be exposed to by such an expression of who they really are? Can they foster a balance of male and female expression in the classroom that might model a better balance out in the world? Can they insist that imagination and eloquence and the world of emotion and sensuality are part of the whole educational process? And that the brain works better in conjunction with the body and the heart than split off from them? Can they cope with truth-telling?

The classroom is one important site for vocal revolution. The home is clearly another. In the home, for women who have daughters, the critical issue is how to reverse traditional upbringing without creating monsters. Can mothers join with their daughters, re-sounding their voices and amplifying the truths they tell? Can mothers bring their daughters up to be emotional democrats? Can mothers and daughters create their own resonant sound-houses that do not depend on male approbation for validation and, at the same time, are not sealed off from, or sound-proofed against, the male vibration?

This puts a huge load on mothers. Mothers may be terrified of the magnitude of their children's grief and rage and fear. All they want to do is hush them, make them stop. In their bones they know the danger. What else can they do? The ear-splitting, mind-bludgeoning screams of a small child when in the throes of a tantrum are variously frightening, enraging or embarrassing. If the mother can hold and soothe the child, the tantrum may pass. Otherwise, the adventurous mother could try joining the child in its emotional universe and, instead of trying to overpower the child with commands, prohibitions and adult superiority, physically get down to the child's level and vocally enter the child's pitch and range. The sound will help her know what her child is feeling as she feels it too through her own voice. Then she can devise a partnership method, a buddy system, for emotional management. They can find a way to come down to earth and ground themselves together.

This may be difficult to do in a public place such as a supermarket – but think of it as a noisy game, no more embarrassing than the common scene where the child snatches a bag of sweets from the shelf and the mother says 'Put that back!' The child refuses, screaming 'I want it, I want it, I want it.' The mother says 'Do what I told you, you're a bad boy/girl.' The child shrieks 'No no no!' Then the mother yells 'Shut up or you know what you'll get' and raises her hand, the child shrieks louder and the mother hits the child.

If a mother has the courage to engage with a child's emotional power, channelling it without crushing it, endorsing the eloquence that comes with it, she can preserve the power of that child's life-force and, in a daughter's case, send her into the world with a dowry beyond price: confidence in the validity of her emotions and a clear sense of her right to speak.

Mothers and daughters are entering an unknown territory when they begin to play together in the emotional realm, relying on empathic give and take rather than accepted rules of parental authority and the old chestnut 'Mother knows best'. Breathing together, voicing feelings, talking endlessly, listening endlessly, could open up new ways for women to be fully present in the world.

There are no precedents for what it means for a woman to have a full, free voice in the world we live in today. The questions remain. Will I be alone if I express myself freely? If I say what I want, will I get what I don't want? How do I remain true to myself and still be a part of society? These are the questions that arose at every workshop for women that Carol Gilligan and I presented under the title *In Our Own Voices*, an outreach from The Company of Women, an all-female Shakespeare company she and I co-directed from 1990 to 1996.

As often as possible we set up weekend theatre camps for girls between the ages of 9 and 13 to coincide with the weekend workshops for women. The theatre camps allowed girls and women to play with each other through theatre games and Shakespeare scenes, with the overall objective of supporting the strength and clarity of girls' voices. In the course of the women's workshops, a combination of voice, theatre and writing exercises, including some autobio-graphical storytelling, gave the women a chance to rediscover some of the strength and clarity they too had possessed as girls. These workshops helped women to recover a resilience, a sense of adventure, an energy and a voice they had lost. The inspiration of the girls built sound-houses for the women to recall their original selves.

In these workshops women combined freewriting and speaking exercises. Over the years, these produced some remarkable fragments of prose and poetry. In the course of a workshop, within a carefully designed framework of breathing, basic voice work, singing, small group and whole group discussions, Carol would give participants the first line for a piece of freewritten prose or poetry about the girls we once were. I reproduce here (with permission from the authors) some writings that arose from these exercises. They signpost a world where the exuberance, joy and energy innate in girls can be unleashed in women when they free their natural voices.

We set up a visualisation in which our 9, 10 or 11-year-old girl self took us on an adventure. 'I want to take you on an adventure,' she says, and we go along with her, eyes closed, wherever she leads, and come back to record the experience.

With my new orange bike really big orange leaving the camp site going faster and faster along the river on the pavement but there down the river warm but the wind cold blowing in my face my hair behind faster & faster no fear pedaling with power my body's power the bike

big & bright & orange & me big on the bike & river big
& the river faster & me faster & orange & bright & wild
& alone me & the river & the orange bike

Patricia Delorey

After the adventure, after listening for her voice as we
explored the stretch of our lives between 7 and 17, we
would freewrite a poem instigated by the line: 'And she
came to tell me...'

And she came to tell me
not to fear my nightmares
she will hold my hand
she tells me
'SING OUT!'
'Sing out Louise!'
You are in the pink
Your cheeky-cheeks giggling
Your belly-big bellowing
Blow Your Horn... She tells me
Your Brass, Your Bold, Your Breasts,
Your Hooters-Toot-Tooters
Let it Rip, Raw and Resonant,
Resilient and Ripe, Rare and Racy
And she tells me
She revels in my revealing
She tells me, she hears me
My heart
My deep inside
My longing
My journey
My voice

Carole Jean Anderson

The writing exercise that wrapped up the archaeological
sonogramming through layers of civilisation to the bedrock

wisdom and energy of the girl began with the line, 'And I heard you say...'

And I heard you say,
Let me be wild and tangled and free
Let me run and yell and catch things
And come back dirty and shining, with thistles in my hair.
I am tired of being timid, you said.
I am tired of being quietly, perfectly creative.
I want to leave my closet door open at night
I want to climb out the window of who I am expected to be
And leap into the reality of wishes, landing in a cascade of
cherry blossoms.

Miriam Rubinow

And I heard you say...
That the girl had always known
What the woman had forgotten
That girl, you girl, my girl
Me girl, an awkward turn
Reversed a hot grill
Like sizzling ham in a skillet
I've been deep-fried into a woman
My juices trapped in breading
My delicate flavor lost in gravy
Now hoping to be wonderfully devoured
A loving juice an angry spice
Boldly savored by a courageous palate
Empty, full, empty, full,
No more self conscious than the impulse.

Suzanne Case

All of the writing and exploration in these workshops was stimulated by practical work on the voice: breathing and physical release work, tongue-stretching, throat-opening, vibrations discovered all over the body, thumping vibrations out from chests, backs, legs and arms, vibrations resonating through the spaces of the ribcage, the face, the skull and out into the room and the world. We played with words from Shakespeare:

O that my tongue were in the thunder's mouth,
Then with a passion would I shake the world.

Constance, *King John*

I hold my peace, sir?
No! I will speak as liberal as the air!
Let heaven, and men, and devils, let them all,
All, all cry shame upon me yet I'll speak.

Emilia, *Othello*

'A Poem to My Voice' was the final workshop exercise. Here are three samples.

If the depth of my feelings
matched the depth of my voice,
If I remember the knowledge
of sound, pure and full,
If I stay connected to
my breath and stand tall,
If I keep my channels open,
will I still be a woman?

Adrienne Cugini

Inside this self-contained shell
                        sits the purloined pearl
45 degrees southwest of the heart
                        She charts her course
through the passions and rages
                        it sends down upon her.
Persistently pressing beyond the censors and sanctions of
'Civilized' society   Struggling to articulate
                What is still unarticulatable.

Gently   Firmly   She weaves her way with words,
     Languishing in language   that can not say
          all she wants it to say
yet.

                    Sandra Balaban

in that darkness that was her voice
she stood
in the center
in the buried pool
it was her heart she heard whisper
far below the surface
it was that great force knocking
from without & within
to which she wished to surrender
it was her voice
rising
it was the thunder
speaking
it was a hand
& a hand
& a hand
reaching
it was a heart
& a heart
& a heart
beating
it was women
it was wonder
it was what she had always been
searching for

                    Phoenix

I think these poems have fundamental pitch.

Bibliography

Carson, Anne, *Glass and God*, Jonathan Cape, London, 1998

Gilligan, Carol, *In a Different Voice*, Harvard University Press, Cambridge, Mass, 1982

—, *Between Voice and Silence: Women and Girls, Race and Relationship*, Harvard University Press, Cambridge, Mass, 1997

Gleason, Maud, W, *Making Men: Sophists and Self-Presentation in Ancient Rome*, Princeton University Press, Princeton, NJ, 1995

Hall, Nor, *The Moon and the Virgin*, The Women's Press, London, 1980

—, *Those Women*, Spring Publications, Dallas, Texas, 1988

Shakespeare, William, *Antony and Cleopatra*, Clarendon Press, Oxford, 1994

Shapcote, Emily, Mary, *Mary: The Perfect Woman*, privately printed by John Griffin, Roehampton, 1903

Transforming Texts
The Power of Shakespeare's Heroines

Cicely Berry

The following is the summary of a conversation I had with Jenny Pearson on the subject of women's voices in Shakespeare. Jenny's questions were very stimulating and our conversation was free-ranging, but it made me think afresh about a number of things. I hope my answers below will prove useful in this way for you.

My work with people's voices has always been linked with speaking text, and by this I mean not just with how the voice sounds when speaking, but with what happens when that sound is released into words: a poem, a speech from a play, and particularly Shakespeare – that is what interests me. I say Shakespeare because there's an energy that comes from the words in his writing which has the power to resonate with a person's inner being, the inner landscape, in a very direct way – and then you can get the most extraordinary transformations.

I remember doing a Shakespeare workshop in the psychiatric ward of a closed hospital: we were working on scenes from *King Lear* and focusing particularly on scenes between Lear and Cordelia. A young woman volunteered to read and I remember her so vividly: she had taken on the part of Cordelia but she had very little voice and was so nervous that she couldn't even read the words out loud. To start with I had to give her the words, ie I read them first and she would speak them after me. Then, very gradually, she got the confidence to read them for herself: what happened after that was just indescribable. We came to the scene towards the end of the play after Cordelia returns to England to rescue her father from her cruel sisters – and his madness – and says:

> Had you not been their father, these white flakes
> Did challenge pity of them . . .

It was deeply moving: she had forgotten all about being nervous, the words came out with authority and with such a sense of being present in them. There was a sense of profound understanding – you felt she owned those words.

I think there is a reason why working with a heightened, poetic text, as compared with a contemporary and more naturalistic text, can get through to people in this way. If you give somebody the opportunity to speak language that is very different from their own, as Shakespeare's is, but that is also very accessible, then it can touch off something in the person – a response to the ideas, to the music of the language – that will take the speaker by surprise. I am talking about very deep feelings being articulated. Suddenly this releases something in the speaker which gives that person confidence. To be able to speak language that has a heightened sound and rhythm gives you a certain sense of power within yourself: and this power is not dangerous, for one is being taken out of oneself and opened up to other feelings. This is what I believe in.

Words have an extraordinary power. I'm not talking about psychological power, but a power beyond what we often recognise – the power of the music of words. It brings about a kind of inner release. If you put people in touch with this experience, extraordinary things can happen and it is my belief that this is how rhetoric originally grew up in primitive societies. People became aware that there were certain forms of sounds which were very powerful and which made an emotional connection: as civilisations developed, these sounds evolved into words. Poetry, and particularly Shakespeare, contains these elements, in which people connect through the sound to something deep down in themselves. When I am working with people I try to put them in touch with that area of language. What then happens to the voice often surprises them: they are surprised by that sound, that vibration, which seems to connect with their feelings and thoughts. And I always find myself moved by the particular way that person comes alive in the role.

There is always a paradox involved in doing this kind of work with a text, whether it is with trained actors or people who have never worked with their voices before: and this paradox is to do with exploring the intention of the character through the argument she/he uses – its logic – and then letting this go to allow the sound of the language to reach the audience without pushing it. We have to open out the depth and thought of a character without overstressing, or explaining or being overemphatic: to speak is to define, and that is enough. The actor is always moving between these two positions – making the sense clear, yet letting the sound be free.

The way I achieve this, to keep the whole thing alive, is not to let it get too serious: to try to surprise people so that they do not have a chance to become self-conscious and tense when working, or to feel there is a 'right' way of speaking poetry – this deadens. Yet of course there is a form we have to honour, there are rhythms, there is music in the language, but once we try consciously to obey 'the rules' we lose our own reality. After all, the dilemma of the actor today in playing Shakespeare, or any heightened poetic text for that matter, is to be able to honour this form and this music, and this extravagant imagery, yet make it feel truthful for now – for today's world. And we must not belittle that imagery, for those images are expressing something so big in character – earth shifts almost.

So over the years I have evolved many different exercises in order to help actors enter the extravagant language without becoming self-conscious: exercises that involve people physically – walking around the room, jostling one another, picking up books that I have thrown on the floor – as they read text aloud. Physical movement keeps people breathing in a full-bodied way, which is essential to get the voice really sounding out. Specific movements, like swinging an arm or jumping on a chair, or changing direction at every punctuation mark, can be used to create emphasis in an organic way without having to think about it. If you can take people's attention away from the text by asking them to draw something simple and specific – for example, what they can see out of the window, or the first house they lived in – they stop worrying about making its 'meaning' clear, and they start speaking the words in such a way that it takes them to new levels of experience. Of course, we have to be clear in our minds about the sense, but that must not stop us from hearing what the words are doing under the language. It is when you become too conscious of your voice, when you focus on it too intensely, that fear takes over and the freedom to connect with this at a deep level is lost – for as I have suggested we can relate to sound at a deeper level than I think we believe.

Voice work is a matter of finding a way past people's fears and defences, connecting them with the full potential of their voice. There are all sorts of reasons why one person's voice may be inhibited and another's relatively expressive and free. Our voices start to be formed very early in our lives, and so one's connection with one's family is possibly the strongest influence – it is of the essence. It is not just about being encouraged or discouraged by one's parents: it is also to do with whether you come from a large family or a small one, a verbal family or a quiet one, whether you are the oldest, the youngest, or somewhere in the middle. And of course the complexities of class structures and status are inextricably mixed with all this. But perhaps the most important issue for the actor is not so definable, for it has to do with one's ear for the sound of language, and this is different for each person: just as some people feel drawn towards music, so others have a relish for the spoken word.

In early childhood the voice is the only connection between your inner person and the outside world. Later, as you grow and start taking charge of yourself, you realise that it is your voice that allows you to communicate with other people – it gives you, or prevents you from having, power. And so you begin to manipulate your voice as a means of getting what you want. This is where gender politics can take its toll: a girl who has grown up with the idea that a 'gentle' voice is more 'attractive' to men may suddenly become vocally inhibited. This was very much so when I was young, but thank goodness it is a position no longer held generally; however, gender politics do not change that quickly and one still comes across women who find it very difficult to assert any kind of vocal power and make themselves heard.

To work with this kind of inhibition and find a way through it, I find it necessary to concentrate first on technical exercises to release the sound, and then, if possible, to get people to do some quite rough physical exercises while speaking which will release that vocal energy that has been suppressed and made to behave. When this energy is released you can get in touch with the aggressiveness of the language – for while you are still speaking you are still asserting your point of view. We have to find this primal need to speak and to express: ie to survive.

The story of women being repressed, silenced, kept away from the action is as old as history – but so are the stories of women who defy the men and the social conventions that seek to disempower them, who insist on living their lives fully in spite of discouragement. These heroines are celebrated in many a traditional song and story all over the world and by no one more than Shakespeare. He had an extraordinary understanding of how it feels to be a woman, as he had of most other things. So when women come to work with Shakespearean texts, connecting through voice work with these vividly articulated feelings, they are frequently surprised into discovering their own strength and aspects of themselves that were not known to them before.

Cordelia is a key role for women discovering and learning to trust the inner strength that comes of being in touch with one's feelings, with one's own true centre. She says 'No' at the very beginning when her father requires her to 'prove' her love for him with verbal flattery and her silence results in banishment. She doesn't return until very nearly the end of the play when the simple, unstated truth of her love for him is proved by her horrified reaction to the way her 'loving' sisters have behaved. She comes back to take care of him.

Rosalind is another Shakespearean heroine; living at her uncle's court, she defies his tyranny and goes away to live in the forest. To travel more safely she dresses and acts as a young man. She gets really high on the experience of taking responsibility for her own safety and that of her cousin Celia, who accompanies her. She emerges from the experience with armour in her system. The role of Rosalind is hugely empowering to actresses, I have seen this again and again. When Rosalind meets Orlando, who loves her but does not recognise her in her manly attire, she has a wonderful time teasing him in spite of the fact that she is also wildly in love with him. She truly takes charge of the situation – and her own destiny.

Ophelia takes up the same theme as Cordelia: she goes against her father's wishes in her relationship with Hamlet, but with a tragic outcome. She eventually goes mad because nobody listens to her or cares what she feels.

She is set up by Polonius and Claudius to meet Hamlet privately: they hide behind the arras in order to hear her exchange with Hamlet, for they want to assess the cause of Hamlet's seeming madness. After her tragically painful encounter and believing Hamlet to be mad, she speaks her thoughts aloud: her soliloquy is one of the most moving speeches in Shakespeare. When she says: 'Oh what a noble mind is here o'erthrown...' who will listen to her – it is a totally male culture. I have often done the following exercise in a workshop: I ask someone to read the speech while the rest of the group walk briskly round the room. When she tries to make somebody listen to what she is saying, they have to turn away and refuse to listen. So – nobody hears her and that is what sends Ophelia mad. That male culture is reinforced a few lines later when Polonius says to her:

> You need not tell us what Lord Hamlet said,
> We heard it all...

Shakespeare has this capacity to see the world from the viewpoint of a woman. Today the subject of women dressing up as men has strong contemporary significance, throwing an interesting light on gender issues. Even dressed as men, Shakespeare's women think like women. Working on *Twelfth Night* recently, with Viola, it was so clear that even though she looks like a boy, she has a woman's perspective inside. This is what makes it so moving. What often makes it difficult for women to articulate anything is that they can usually see the whole perspective of their problem, they see all round it, whereas a man will see an angle on it and focus on that. This often makes women less emphatic than men in how they express themselves and people interpret this as not being confident – but it is not so!

When Viola goes to woo Olivia on Orsino's behalf, she

begins her task by speaking what she believes would be his words, which do not impress Olivia at all. Then she gets lost in her own feelings for Orsino and her 'willow cabin' speech moves Olivia. Olivia responds because Viola's words are real, they come from a deep place – the feelings of a 'disguised' woman in love with the man whose message she has come to deliver. Olivia believes that she is falling in love with a young man, but she is actually falling in love with a kind of dream – a woman's fantasy of a man who understands love in the way a woman does. This is the dream-like centre of Shakespeare's most romantic comedy. Viola's words touch the very core of our capacity to love as women. If we speak the words, allow them to take hold of us as we speak Shakespeare's words, we make a powerful connection with our own capacity to love.

I will end by quoting the four passages I have referred to in this chapter so that you can experiment with my approach to finding the meaning and the energy of Shakespeare through vocal work with the text. It is, as I think we all recognise, very difficult to convey the ex- perience of voice work by writing about it on the page, for so much depends on the kind of personal encouragement you get when working within a group in a real physical space. But you may find, if you set about sounding the words out, exploring them in a way that is not too serious, perhaps moving about the room and engaging physically with their sound, that it will reinforce and enrich this connection with language that I have been talking about. This can happen at all levels of experience.

From *Hamlet*

Ophelia   O, what a noble mind is here o'erthrown!
        The courtier's, soldier's, scholar's, eye, tongue, sword,
        Th'expectancy and rose of the fair state,

The glass of fashion and the mould of form,
Th'observ'd of all observers, quite, quite down!
And I, of ladies most deject and wretched,
That suck'd the honey of his music vows,
Now see that noble and most sovereign reason
Like sweet bells jangled, out of tune and harsh;
That unmatched form and feature of blown
    youth
Blasted with ecstasy. O, woe is me
T'have seen what I have seen, see what I see.

From *King Lear*

Cordelia   O, my dear father! Restoration hang
    Thy medicine on my lips; and let this kiss
    Repair those violent harms that my two
        sisters
    Have in thy reverence made.

Kent   Kind and dear Princess!

Cordelia   Had you not been their father, these white
        flakes
    Did challenge pity of them. Was this a face
    To be oppos'd against the jarring winds?
    To stand against the deep dread bolted
        thunder,
    In the most terrible and nimble stroke
    Of quick cross lightning? To watch, poor
        perdu,
    With this thin helm? Mine enemy's dog
    Though he had bit me, should have stood that
        night
    Against my fire; and wast thou fain, poor
        father,
    To hovel thee with swine and rogues forlorn

In short and musty straw? Alack, alack!
'Tis wonder that thy life and wits at once
Had not concluded all.

From *As You Like It*

Orlando   Where dwell you, pretty youth?

Rosalind   With this shepherdess, my sister, here in the skirts of the forest, like fringe upon a petticoat.

Orlando   Are you native of this place?

Rosalind   As the cony that you see dwell where she is kindled.

Orlando   Your accent is something finer than you could purchase in so removed a dwelling.

Rosalind   I have been told so of many; but indeed an old religious uncle of mine taught me to speak, who was in his youth an inland man, one that knew courtship too well, for there he fell in love. I have heard him read many lectures against it, and I thank God I am not a woman, to be touch'd with so many giddy offences as he hath generally tax'd their whole sex withal.

Orlando   Can you remember any of the principal evils that he laid to the charge of women?

Rosalind   There were none principal, they were all like one another as halfpence are, every one fault seeming monstrous till his fellow-fault came to match it.

Orlando   I prithee, recount some of them.

Rosalind   No; I will not cast away my physic but on those that are sick. There is a man haunts the forest that abuses our young plants with carving 'Rosalind' on their barks;

hangs odes upon hawthorns, and elegies on brambles; all, forsooth, deifying the name of Rosalind. If I could meet that fancy-monger, I would give him some good counsel, for he seems to have the quotidian of love upon him.

Orlando   I am he that is so love-shak'd, I pray you, tell me your remedy.

Rosalind   There is none of my uncle's marks upon you. He taught me how to know a man in love; in which cage of rushes you are not prisoner.

Orlando   What were his marks?

Rosalind   A lean cheek, which you have not; a blue eye and sunken, which you have not; an unquestionable spirit, which you have not; a beard neglected, which you have not – but I pardon you for that, for simply your having in beard is a younger brother's revenue. Then your hose should be ungarter'd, your bonnet unbanded, your sleeve unbutton'd, your shoe untied, and everything about you demonstrating a careless desolation. But you are no such man; you are rather point-device in your accoutrements, as loving yourself than seeming the lover of any other.

Orlando   Fair youth, I wish I could make thee believe I love.

Rosalind   Me believe it? You may as soon make her that you love believe it, which, I warrant, she is apter to do than confess she does. That is one of the points in the which women still give the lie to their consciences. But in good sooth, are you he that hangs the verses on the trees where Rosalind is so admired?

From *Twelfth Night*

Viola	If I did love you in my master's flame
	With such a suff'ring, such a deadly life,
	In your denial I would find no sense;
	I would not understand it.
Olivia	Why, what would you?
Viola	Make me a willow cabin at your gate,
	And call upon my soul within the house:
	Write loyal cantons of contemned love
	And sing them loud even in the dead of night;
	Halloo your name to the reverberate hills,
	And make the babbling gossip of the air
	Cry out 'Olivia!' O, you should not rest
	Between the elements of air and earth,
	But you would pity me!

Bibliography

Berry, Cicely, *The Actor and the Text*, Harrap, London, 1987, (revised edition 1993). I have written extensively about these exercises in this book, which deals with how modern acting approaches can relate to heightened language.

—*Voice and the Actor*, Harrap, London, 1973. My first book, which deals with all aspects of voice training for the actor.

—*Your Voice and How to Use It*, Virgin Books, London, 1974. My second book, written primarily for public speakers, has recently been updated to include interviews with Neil Kinnock, Helena Kennedy and Tariq Ali.

The Voice of African-American Women

Ysaye M Barnwell

By birth, I am African-American and female. By training, I am a speech pathologist and a public health educator. By the grace of God, I am a singer. And by destiny, I am honoured to be a member of Sweet Honey in the Rock. Each of these aspects of my being has a place in this piece about the voice of African-American women.

Early in my training as a speech pathologist I read a textbook in which Dr Wendell Johnson stated that 'The voice is the barometer of the soul'. I have grown to understand and appreciate the truth of this statement. Recently Toi Derricotte, another African-American woman, wrote in her book *The Black Notebooks: An interior journey*:

> Coming to one's voice is...not a linear process, not a matter of learning skills, forms, and laws of grammar and syntax. It is a dynamic process in which much of what is occurring and has occurred remains inside.

She was writing about the writer's voice, although her statement can as easily be read as applying to the voice with which we literally make ourselves heard. The emergence of one's voice involves much more than the linear process of learning vocal technique, developing and preserving one's instrument, choosing and learning a repertoire and going on the concert platform or stage. It is a process, often gradual, of 'bearing' – of giving birth to – one's soul: the ancestral, spiritual, cultural, social, political and psychological influences and processes that allow one's true voice to emerge. This is particularly true for women, as well as for other groups considered a 'minority' within a society which tends, as a matter of course, to want to silence you or make you invisible.

How shall we, here, define 'voice', which can at the same time express itself through speech or song; spiritually, through prayer; emotionally, through a cry or a laugh; silently, through the mighty pen; politically, through the ballot; socially, through the privilege of birth; and financially, through the dollar – or, indeed, any other currency?

I would like to define 'voice' as 'the expression of personal and/or communal power' and 'the courage to fill whatever space you choose to be in'. That space may be a sheet of paper – the space where only your thoughts abide – a room, or a nation's conscience.

The voices of African-American women are rooted in Africa and shaped by the experience of slavery in America. Held in these roots is a world view which continues to inform our communal voices. And there are some fundamental characteristics of African-American music which grow out of these same roots.

The first of these characteristics has to do with *functionality*. It has been said that when art is understood by everyone, it ceases to be art. Within this context it is easy to understand that in traditional cultures and societies 'art', as we experience it in the Western world today, did not exist. Music, dance, poetry, carvings, drawings, pottery and textiles were all necessities within the culture. Everyone participated in using these tools because without them life itself would not have been possible. Communication with the invisible, with the higher spiritual powers, with the ancestors, with the as yet unborn, with other forms of life and with the environment would not have been possible. The transmission of knowledge from generation to generation would not have been possible and nor would the conduct of ritual and craft.

Within traditional cultures there are persons who may be selected to develop mastery of a given skill. Such mastery is not achieved for personal glorification but is used to serve the community in prescribed ways. In the modern Western world, art is often something which is elevated above and set apart from the ranks of the masses. In this context, art represents a level of mastery which places the artist in an exclusive world – a world which can usually only be observed in a museum, gallery or concert hall. Because it does not serve a community or a tradition, such art need not be responsible to any community or tradition.

African-Americans have never relinquished functionality as an essential element in our music: it serves the community in concrete ways. As a result, since our arrival in the New World in the 1600s, new musical forms have emerged among us whenever there has been a significant change in our social, political and spiritual circumstances as a people.

Within the experience of slavery, in spite of the fact that slaves had no social, political or financial voice, African-Americans created the *spiritual* – our most powerful and enduring body of songs, which was to inspire and inform all the musical forms that followed it. Spirituals evolved as communities of slaves, with nothing but their voices and inherent rhythm, sought to document and communicate the full impact of slavery on both their individual and collective psyches; the imposing combination of African spirituality and Christianity; the dialectic of remaining enslaved versus escaping to freedom; and their dignity, nobility and pride in the face of inhuman treatment and total despair.

Blues evolved after slavery came to an end and after the

period known as Reconstruction (1865–1877). Blues emerged not as a communal or a sacred voice but as an individual, secular voice as, one by one, people began the Great Migration of Blacks from the southern United States to the states in the north, mid-west and west – particularly during the years between 1911 and 1915.

Gospel music, urban and Christian at its core and bearing the influence of its secular cousins – blues, ragtime and jazz – emerged in the 1920s. This was the time when the migrants – ex-slaves and descendants of slaves – were beginning to assimilate into a world of 'free Negroes' in big cities with big churches, who sang hymns, anthems, cantatas and oratorios, much as the whites did.

The music of the Civil Rights Movement of the 1960s incorporated all the vocal musical forms of the nineteenth and twentieth centuries: spirituals, work songs, hymns, blues, 40s rhythm 'n' blues, rock and roll songs, children's game songs, etc. This music galvanised communities all over the south, while informing communities all over the world about racist activities occurring in the south that were not being reported in northern papers like *The New York Times*. With the change of a word or two, or the creation of new lyrics to familiar melodies, these songs documented incidents, reported names of both perpetrators and victims, and encouraged people to get involved in the movement for civil rights. In the practice of this non-violent movement, the songs became the weapon and shield for those who marched, sat-in, rode buses, went to jail, were beaten and tortured.

More recently, in the 1980s and 1990s, Rap music has signified the rise of a generation still rooted in tradition but shaped by a new set of values and informed by an ever-changing technology. They have given up the melody and gone back to basics with the rhythm. The rhythmic song-speech of the African *griot*, Black preacher and Black orator are all there – again, documenting and deliberating in full public view the issues of the times.

As people of African descent we cannot exist without music. This has been apparent throughout the African diaspora. How can we sing our songs in a strange land? We have to sing to let others know that we are in a strange land, but that we continue to exist.

The second characteristic of African-American music that I want to look at is *poly-rhythms*. At the core of Africa and everywhere in the diaspora is the phenomenon of more than one rhythm happening at a time. Often the rhythms are different, but in the same meter. More exciting is the simultaneous performance of compound rhythms – for example, 6/8 and 4/4 – which are not only complex but very seductive. The successful performance of poly-rhythms, whether simple or compound, requires the respectful listening and co-operation of all the performers. The metaphors to which this concept can be applied are numerous. In this tradition, we are not expected to do the same thing: in fact, the interplay of variety is required. The only way that this can be achieved in a meaningful way is with active listening – first with a sharp, then with a soft focus – and the willingness to be continuously responsive in making the small modifications necessary to remain in synch with every other rhythm. One contemporary example of this concept is the political *coalition* where many organisations, all with their own agendas, come together to work on an issue much larger than any of the individual organisations could tackle alone.

I am struck by the many examples of the poly-rhythm metaphor found in African-American culture. A clear example was the Civil Rights Movement. No matter how you wanted to participate, there was an organisation which could support you. If your major concern was with the legal aspects of Civil Rights, the NAACP (National Association for the Advancement of Colored People) was the legal arm of the movement; if you were a student and practising non-violence, there was the SNCC (Student Non-violent Co-ordinating Committee); if you were church based, there was the SCLC (Southern Christian Leadership Conference). There was CORE (Congress of Racial Equality), The Urban League, the Black Panthers and the Black Muslims. Each of these organisations, and others, held a piece of the puzzle which made up the whole Civil Rights Movement between 1954 and 1968.

Call and response is another characteristic form. For centuries, this oral/aural method of acquiring and transmitting knowledge and information has existed in cultures not dependent on the written word. It is not simply an effective technique for learning the words, rhythms and tunes of a song. It involves an ongoing process for evaluating closer and closer approximations of any expected skill or behaviour. It compels everyone present to participate in some way, obliterating the distinction between performer and audience. Call and response is a primary feature of both African and African-American music. It is practised to a high degree in gospel music in which the congregation, or chorus, must listen for and repeat an ever-changing text that is supplied by the song leader. It is also present in jazz, where one or more musicians must reproduce complicated rhythmic and melodic patterns which are often improvised, initially, by another musician.

Interchangeability of leader and follower is another characteristic. I have heard it said that 'You can accomplish anything if you don't care who gets the credit'. In African and African-American music, it is not uncommon for leadership to change hands or revolve. In jazz the lead may be played first, for example, by the sax, but it may then shift to the trumpet, then the piano, then the bass and on to the drummer, before returning to the sax. In traditional gospel quartet singing, the lead may shift between a tenor lead and a bass lead. In congregational singing, one person may raise a hymn which may be taken or switched to an entirely different song by another person. At a funeral once, I saw a second singer slide in and take over the lead from a singer who was overcome with grief: the change was hardly noticeable and when the original lead regained her composure she reassumed her role. This is exactly as it should be. We each have a role, sometimes as leaders and sometimes as followers. Each supports the other and neither is more important, for one cannot exist without the other.

Improvisation: I often get the feeling that people who are not of African descent look at our musical performance with its unique sense of freedom and feel in their depiction or replication of the style that they can 'do anything'. Nothing could be further from the truth. In much of the music found in Africa and the diaspora, there is much room for spontaneity and improvisation, but it should be remembered that all music has rules. Improvisation occurs within the structure/rules of the music being performed. Depending on the musical form, some elements of the music will be strictly prescribed and must be performed without variation, while others allow for or require improvisation. The form of the music will define the rules for the improvisation. Viewed from another perspective, the musician/singer is a medium whose skill may be knowing how and when to get out of the way of *spirit*. The song must be sung until it sings itself. On the one hand, improvisation is a conscious process applied to a given theme and, on the other, it is a spiritual moment which transforms the experience.

All the factors I have been describing shape, and have shaped, the voice of African-American women. During slavery Harriet Tubman, an escaped slave and leader of the 'underground railroad', used her voice in song to announce her presence, to signal danger and to give encouragement to those who had the courage to journey to freedom. Over time, she enlarged the space occupied by an increasing number of escaped slaves so that it stretched from the southern United States all the way to Canada. Sojourner Truth, also an escaped slave, used both her songs and powerful oratory to speak the truth (as her chosen name suggested) for civil rights and women's rights. These women of the nineteenth century gained enormous personal power: they gained *voice*. One hundred years after the Emancipation Proclamation they were paralleled in the twentieth century, most notably by women like Fanny Lou Hamer[1], Shirley Chisholm[2] and Barbara Jordan[3], women of enormous personal and political power, who literally took the space they needed and filled it with their voices. These voices created space for other voices as well.

Rosalyn M Story, in the introduction to her book *And So I Sing – African-American Divas of Opera and Concert*, states:

> From the first diva, Elizabeth Taylor-Greenfield, to the modern artist, the black opera singer has achieved as much by changing the face of classical music in the last century as black women who pioneered for civil rights. Just as Rosa Parks anchored the movement for equality in Montgomery and Ida B Wells Barnett fought against the evil of lynching in the South, Marian Anderson and the great artists who preceded her forged a new order in a world where black voices were often ignored and, at best, severely underrated.

Many, if not most, American musicians and singers are trained first in the Black Church, consciously and unconsciously learning a vast repertoire of spirituals, common long and short meter hymns, traditional and contemporary gospel songs, as well as anthems and cantatas. It is from this cultural base that the African-American musician/singer will venture into training in the European classical tradition.

African-American singers and musicians are often bicultural, performing in both the African-American genres of folk, blues, jazz, pop and gospel, and European classical music. It is not uncommon for an African-American opera singer to affirm her/his cultural and social identity by concluding a performance of European classical music with a group of Negro spirituals. At the 1998 GRAMMY Awards, Aretha Franklin, the undisputed Queen of Soul, when called upon at the last minute to sing the aria 'Nessun Dorma' from Puccini's opera Turandot in place of Pavarotti, did so with stunning finesse. Many classically trained singers and musicians have focused their careers on the more popular genres because they found European classical music to be too inaccessible.

African-American women are often bi-directional, too. We are compelled to serve each other and our communities. We understand, more and more, that we are meant to nourish and nurture ourselves as well. A healthy voice is one which speaks for the self as well as others.

In addition to understanding the characteristics, capabilities and potential of her physical instrument, coming into her voice requires that the singer (and the speaker and writer) acknowledge having inherited, embraced or assumed a cultural and psychological identity. Choice of repertoire, song style, vocal sounds, quality, texture and an acceptable range of voice are culturally determined or influenced. But the degree to which a woman can accept her voice as her own and not that of someone else, and the degree to which she is willing to be truthful and vulnerable – these factors are psychologically and/or spiritually determined. As we compose and live our lives, so we prepare ourselves for the songs we must sing. We cannot ignore the voices of our mothers and grandmothers. We take them with us as we move into tomorrow.

Notes

1. Fanny Lou Hamer, who was spokesperson for the Freedom Democratic Party at the 1964 national Democratic convention, changed the course of political events in the state of Mississippi.
2. Shirley Chisholm was America's first Black Congresswoman and, in 1972, was the first African-American woman to bid for presidential nomination by the Democratic Party.
3. Barbara Jordan became a United States congresswoman in 1972 and gained notoriety in 1974 for her articulate and impassioned speech at the impeachment hearing of Richard Nixon. She gave the keynote address at both the 1976 and 1995 national Democratic conventions.

Publications

Barnwell, Ysaye M, ed, *Continuum: The First Songbook of Sweet Honey in the Rock*, Sweet Honey in the Rock Contemporary A Capella Press, Maine, 2000

—*No Mirrors in My Nana's House*, illustrated by Synthia Saint James, Harcourt Brace, London, 1998

Singing in the African-American Tradition, taught by Dr Ysaye Barnwell with Dr George Brandon. An instructional set of six tapes or four CDs with a manual, Homespun Tapes, Woodstock, NY

Bodies Under Siege

Frankie Armstrong

Listen – Look:

Obstacles, diminishing, loss, weakness, deteriorating, limitations, stress, distressed, excruciating pain, contraction, restricted, fear, frustration, doldrums.

Listen – Look:

Free, fun, joy, release, empowering, uninhibited, spontaneous, healing, strength, sustained, beautiful, share, truth, homecoming, liberation, relief, connected, kinship, energy.

I have selected these words from the contributions that make up this chapter. How is it that the experiences captured by the first list can be transformed into the second? At its core it is a mystery with a very strong physical underpinning. The body, the senses, even when under siege, can still enliven and find and release energy. Hence we have a very embodied mystery which, as you will see, has given the women in this chapter something of inestimable value. Initially I planned to write about women with disabilities but, as I talked to friends and colleagues, it became clear that there is a wider set of circumstances where the body is restricted, constrained and stressed, so I broadened the contributions to include childbirth, illness, accident and death. Most of the contributors are known to me personally and this means they are not a random group but rather those who I knew had something direct and powerful to say about their experience. However, I am sure they are representative of a much larger and wider group of women who have used their voices to creatively transform the experience of bodies under siege.

My Story – My Song

Out of the darkness comes the fear of what's to come,
Out of the darkness comes the dread of what's undone,
Out of the darkness comes the hope that we can run
And out of the darkness comes the knowledge of the
    sun.

Out of the darkness comes the fear of the unknown,
Out of the darkness comes the dread of bleaching
    bone,
Out of the darkness comes the hope we're not alone
And out of the darkness grow the seeds that we have
    sown.

Out of the darkness comes the fear, revenge and hate,
Out of the darkness comes the dread of indifferent
    fate,
Out of the darkness comes the hope we're not too late
And out of the darkness come the songs that we
    create.

Darkness is the place of birth, darkness is the womb,
Darkness is the place of rest, darkness is the tomb,
Darkness belongs to life, half of day is night,
We need not fear the darkness but a blinding flash of
    light.

I wrote this song at the time of the encirclement of Greenham Cruise Missile Base by the Women's Peace Camp, inspired by their courage and actions. I was also inspired by the words of Euripides (John Barton's translation) from over 2000 years ago telling of Apollo's ascendancy over the Pythoness in the dark oracular cave at Delphi: 'And now our aching hearts no longer understand the truth in the night. We only listen to Apollo and the light.'

I'm not sure whether the fact that I was losing my sight had any bearing on my writing this. However, I was faced, as are any of us with little or no sight, with a linguistic and imagistic world that seemed to glorify the light and denigrate the dark. Saint Paul most famously etched this moralistic notion onto Christian history. The Women's Movement and post Jungian women psychologists were among those who began to challenge this. And above (or should I say 'below'?) all, it was the voice and song that taught me to respect the dark, the unseen, the unknown.

In houses, streets, buses and tubes, I might find myself bumped, pushed, bruised; no matter how skilled a user of the long cane I became, hedges and scaffolding at head height were a threat and a menace. The world was an increasingly unsafe place and yet, paradoxically, my life was growing richer and more satisfying. In 1987, three years before I was to regain some sight through a miraculous operation at Moorfields Eye Hospital in London, I had almost no functional sight left when I wrote:

There is vision not sensed by sight, an insight born of
    loss and grieving,
To face the darkness, face the night,
Brings lightness and a heart's rejoicing.
It was a wise seer who broke the ties
When he said 'I see through, not with my eyes.'

(The wise seer was William Blake.)

It is no accident that I wrote this as a song and not a

poem. It is the act of singing that has transformed my life and given me the energy, passion and joy with which to encourage others to experience this for themselves. Darkness can be turned into a heart's rejoicing, into lightness. Singing is the bridge from the inner dark out into the space around – even if that space is not experienced as light (as it was not for me, for many years, and is not for many visually impaired people).

To sense one's voice soaring, spiralling, cutting through that space, is to inhabit it in ways that are impossible either visually or physically. As you read on through this chapter you will doubtless be struck by the number of times contributors describe the sense of freedom singing allows. Running, leaping, swinging – things that may be impossible for the wheelchair user or the profoundly physically restricted – are all captured through the voice and singing.

It has me wondering if maybe I have been blessed with the best of both worlds despite having apparently been largely robbed of one. As a child I wanted to follow in my mother's footsteps as a visual artist or designer and it was my best subject at school. As soon as I could I was splotching paper and I continued to paint and sketch throughout my childhood and youth. As it later transpired, I must have had my eye condition from before the age when I could hold a paintbrush. By pure fluke – or destiny, according to one's perspective – it was just as my sight first started to deteriorate noticeably that I began to sing in public with a local skiffle group, out in rural Hertfordshire where I was brought up. It was modest beginnings, but we took the music seriously and listened to the great blues and folk singers such as Bessie Smith and Woody Guthrie. And whatever I sang, I threw my whole being into it: why else do it? As it became clear, despite correct diagnosis and treatment at last, that my sight would worsen, not improve, my love of music overtook my passion for art.

Hence for me it became easier and easier to focus on what it was I *could* do as opposed to what I couldn't (as Monica Redden also points out).

And yet I continued to have a strong visual imagination. Even when I had little or no sight I would be able to tell you, after a visit to the theatre, the colour of the hero or heroine's hair or clothes: of course, this was all in my imagination! And I am drawn to songs that conjure up strong colours, pictures and landscapes. Hence I still call upon my strong visual sense to give colour to the voice and nuance to the interpretation of songs. One reviewer has said of my singing '...she paints a series of pictures which, if any one were done with half the effect by a film maker, would bring in a string of Oscars' (Bob Harrington, *Taplas*).

I feel that it was the loss of sight that helped me to develop this ability. It gave me a passion for the voice and a ferocious capacity to attend to the unending range of expression of which it is capable.

Some months after regaining some sight (while, however, remaining legally blind) I was faced with another restriction as the hearing of one ear was considerably damaged. This has made socialising in public places such as restaurants or pubs with 'background' music so difficult as to be no longer pleasurable. Sighted people use visual clues all the time to augment hearing in such contexts, which I can't do – so, without these and with the barrage of constant noise that seems to accompany our modern lives, I find myself excluded from the camaraderie and spontaneity which at best accompany social events. But the context in which like-souled people come together to sing or listen to song still gives me the possibility of sharing in this sociability to the full, without loss of sight and hearing being defining factors. So while life is full of myriad petty frustrations and inconveniences, these are more than balanced by the most enormous blessings and satisfactions.

The women below tell their stories of pain, grief, frustration, fear and limitation, and how they, like me, have found the transformational power of voice and song. It seems fitting to begin at the beginning, with Suzanne Chawner telling of the natural birth of her first child.

'You're going to have a really sore throat tomorrow,' Rachel, the midwife, said to me.

'Oh no, I'm not,' I replied. 'I was using Frankie Armstrong's method of voice production!'

She stared at me blankly.

This incongruous exchange took place as Rachel left me at seven in the morning, following a labour which began at seven the previous evening and ended with the birth of my daughter Eleanor in a birthing pool at St Mary's, Paddington, at 4am. Nine hours of the most excruciating pain known to humankind. And I coped with nothing but the encouragement of two midwives, my husband Phil and my friend Louise, the warm water of the birthing pool to relax in between contractions, and making an extraordinary variety of sounds at the top of my voice whenever the contractions came.

My friend Louise had been with a lot of women in labour (she used to be a midwife) and told me she had never heard a woman make as much noise as I did! She said it was just as well I had chosen to give birth in a hospital, because if I'd stayed home they would have heard me from the top of the nearby hill! I remember, in one of Frankie's workshops, pretending to be a shepherd calling across the valley and then using the technique to actually call across a wonderful valley in the Yorkshire dales. Well, this time they would have heard me across the next valley and in the neighbouring town as well!

Making the sounds really helped. At one point I tried the commonly taught method of 'breathing' through the contraction, but I could see no advantage in not actually expressing the pain when it was happening. The breathing method seemed to involve removing myself one step from the level of pain I was experiencing – and yet I was still very conscious that it was happening. So I soon went back to my creative expression of the pain of labour.

In a sense I enjoyed making the noises I made, perhaps because it gave me a feeling of being in control. I couldn't control the pain coming at me from inside, but I could control the response I made to it. As I felt the contraction coming on, I took a deep breath and made an uninhibited, continuous, high decibel sound from deep inside myself for as long as the contraction lasted. The ones I remember most clearly were a kind of 'oi-oi-oi-oi-oi' sound and an 'ai-ai-ai-ai-ai' sound. The 'ai-ai' came from 'aia!' which is Italian for 'ow!' I can see now that 'ai-ai-ai' is far easier and more satisfying to repeat than 'ow-ow-ow!' And there were plenty of other sounds from foreign languages not known even to myself. I recently asked my husband what he remembered of the noises I made. He said 'When you opened your throat up and really bellowed it was very, very loud!' And I kept this up for nine hours – some work-out!

There was a period that seemed to go on for ever when I was saying between contractions 'I can't do it. It's too much...' And my midwives were saying back 'Yes you can. You ARE doing it!' And then when I really felt the urge to push I could not wait any longer. With two almighty contractions accompanied by the most harrowing screams imaginable, my daughter was born.

In contrast to the high decibel scream that was still dying on the air, Eleanor came up out of the water and whimpered a bit! If anyone had heard the sounds I made in labour they would know for sure how hard it was. I think it would strike you as a violent thing if you heard the screams I made as she was actually born. And yet, for her, it was a gentle birth. She whimpered as she lay on me, then became completely quiet as she lay in my husband's arms while I got out of the pool. A couple of minutes later she was enjoying her first breastfeed.

Making the noises as I did greatly helped me to achieve the birth I wanted for my daughter. I have a strong belief that a gentle birth without pain relief is a wonderful start in life for a baby. It is perhaps ironic that a gentle birth for her entailed me becoming a bit of a savage, emitting the wildest sounds imaginable. The years I had spent singing had really helped to free me of inhibitions about making a noise. I feel I was spontaneously using the technique Frankie teaches: proof that this technique works was that, no, I didn't have a sore throat the next day. And yes, holding Eleanor in my arms for the first time was the most wonderful experience in my life.

But what happens if the pain is equally excruciating but is not going to be over in nine hours or, possibly, ever? Could the experience of using the voice ever capture the sense of delight and relief Suzanne talks of? Here is Liz Hodgson's story:

I was a participant in Frankie's first training week (for people wanting to use her methods in their work) back in 1988. The first Voice Workshop I attended was four or five years before that and it had made a huge impact on my life as well as my voice. It was a kind of homecoming in which I realised that singing wasn't just something I could do: I could develop it, enjoy it, benefit from it and simply *be* the singing. I had run some workshops and started to perform in folk clubs before Frankie's training week. After it, I began to run workshops in Oxford with Nina Chandler, who was also part of that training week.

Some years later the local LETS scheme had a group of people who wanted to get together and sing. They invited me to get something going. The outcome was LETSING, an informal singing session which took place regularly and eventually developed into a series of classes under my direction at the local community arts venue, with some spin-off performances.

I became a mother in 1993. After my son Toby was born, I was getting intermittent pain in my joints. This was diagnosed as a reaction to the massive dose of antibiotics I had been given as treatment for the septicaemia that I contracted when I was in hospital for the birth. The pains returned in 1996 and the GP diagnosed 'osteoarthritis'. My condition became gradually worse, in spite of medication and homeopathy. By August 1997 my limbs were sore all the time. I could barely manage to get out of bed in the mornings or, once I was up, to put one foot in front of the other and walk. I decided to give up my part-time job and send Toby to a free local nursery instead of the paid nursery in town. I felt that I was a wimp and an awful mother. This is what arthritis can do, especially to 'younger onset' people under 45, like myself. It was some time before the NHS came up with the correct diagnosis of rheumatoid arthritis, meaning that my immune system was in chaos and attacking my bones. By this time I was a semi-invalid. When I wasn't limping to school with Toby, resting against walls and yelling at him to stop and wait for me, I was sleeping at every opportunity, scared to cross the road and desperate about my garden, my family and my bank balance.

And yet, throughout this time, I sang. I ran weekly groups. I devised, rehearsed and directed performances with groups of dancers. I ran vocal warm-ups and a workshop for a 70-strong Harmony Weekend, teaching four-part harmony songs on the spot because there was no one else around who could teach songs by ear. I even sang a fragment of an Irving Berlin song for two Butoh dancers who were performing at the local theatre.

How was this possible? I limped on and off stage and had to sit down when running voice workshops. I got lifts so that I wouldn't have to drive. I reflected how good it was that my instrument was so portable, that I wasn't a cellist or a trumpeter. I remember arriving to run a group at 7.30pm saying that I would probably have to leave after an hour – and still being there two hours later. I started the singing series in 1997 with the traditional Zulu song *Ndinani na*, meaning 'What's wrong with me?' from Miriam Makeba's repertoire, learnt from her mother who was a traditional healer. (She describes, in her notes on the song, how it feels to go to the doctor and worry about what his diagnosis will be, a feeling I knew all too well.) We used *Ndinani na* in a performance that December when I was really ill. I still remember letting the call that starts the song ring out in the acoustic of the former church where we were performing. It seemed to be singing *through* me.

In those difficult months I did nothing else in public but sing. I don't think I could have done anything else if I had tried. Standing for an hour to help behind a stall at a school jumble sale was dispiriting and painful, even before I got really bad. But when I was singing I was okay. Is this because I love strutting my stuff? Because I know I can sing? Because I have a physical memory of power and energy associated with resonance? Because singing belongs to my sense of identity and lifts me out of my invalid state? Because it was a voluntary activity and on some occasions I was invited to do it? A group member has told me that in spite of my vulnerability at that time, my singing did something for the group, enabling them to feel more readily what singing was doing for them.

My conclusion is that singing is not merely possible, it can also be positively helpful for someone whose body is under siege as mine was. I don't know exactly how this comes about, but I can hazard a few guesses. It could be partly related to physical processes involved in singing, such as the oxygenating effects of deep breathing. It may be that the resonance itself is beneficial to the body. Certainly the quality of concentration required to keep three or four harmonies in my head at once distracted me from the pain and my work with the groups fed me, in spite of the energy I had to expend, because all the time I was standing or sitting surrounded by sound, buoyed up by it in much the same way as water sustains my body now that I am able to go swimming again. While I encouraged others to sing I was also helping myself.

Looking back over this time, I'm sure that I would have been more ill as well as isolated and even poorer without the singing. The songs I sang and taught to the groups were 'up' songs, positive and vigorous, as compared with the slower, more introspective songs that I gravitate towards as a soloist. Whatever the words, whatever the notes, I know that singing taps into some process that everyday life obscures.

Monica Redden now lives and works in Sydney, though we have also met and sung together in Britain and Hong Kong. Here is Monica's story.

In 1990 I discovered my voice. My discovery came at a time when I was feeling physically constricted and frustrated from the effects of a work related injury. Finding the power of my voice and being able to produce something so wonderful and colourful had a major healing effect. I discovered a strength in me that was now confirmed by body movement. The impact of the realisation that I had power in spite of physical restrictions triggered my thoughts into defining my life in terms of *what I have* as compared with *what I do not have*. This re-frame has sustained me many a time over the years.

I recall an experience several years after the initial shoulder injury when I slipped a disk in my back. I was stuck on an island in a foreign country and there was nobody I knew within screaming distance to help me. There I sat for three hours in the bathroom, unable to move and in excruciating pain, waiting for my partner to come home. My immediate response was fear, 'Oh, no, not another injury!' My second response was to sing. I sat there and created the most stunning harmonic overtones, exploring the full range of sound and colour that only overtones can provide. These overtones continued to sustain me during the weeks of rehabilitation. Again I experienced power and strength that were not dependent on physical movement.

The grinding, relentless pain I experienced with my initial injury led me to restrict my movements in the false belief that the restriction would assist in the healing. In reality, the more I limited my movements, the more I not only limited my physical recovery but also began to constrict and shrink my spirit. Fourteen months after the onset of my injury I felt that the woman who was once vibrant, physically active, strong and confident had been replaced by a sad, under-confident, immobilised woman.

The opening line of a poem I wrote in the midst of my recovery actually prophesied the answer to my state of depression...'*I'm just grovelling on the ground without a sound*'. The rediscovery of my voice has given me more strength than any person could hope to gain from a strong physical body. It has given me the ability to run, soar, swing from trees, float and jump, and to share all this with anybody who wants to listen.

Louise Barchard is a wheelchair-user, which currently means she is denied access to many places that the ambulant take for granted. Louise not only has to contend with these external frustrations, but also with the knowledge and nature of a degenerative condition.

Progressive muscle wasting means that gradually, over many years, my ability to explore wild countryside landscapes has got harder. However, a whole new way of exploring landscapes has opened up to me without leaving the house. In these landscapes I come up against far fewer obstacles and I am less bound by the limitations imposed by my diminished skeletal muscles. It is wonderful to experience the joy of a growing and strengthening physical faculty when what I am used to is recurrent disappointment and loss as my muscles weaken.

I use voice a lot with movement and exercise to help maintain optimal physical functioning. The vocal sound frees and supports my movement, eases tight and aching muscles, massages from within and makes exercising a lot more fun. Sounding my voice enables me to feel 'worked out' when my body is too tired to function in other ways. I have a growing library of sounds and rhythms, from the smallest and softest to the greatest and most raucous. I never quite know what I am going to find in there next. I know that good 'sounding' simultaneously grounds me in my body and makes my body feel lighter and easier to move around. I know that without vocalising life would be a lot harder. It releases tension. Consciously using my breath helps me to relax and freshens my spirit. It also helps me to find stillness. Once the sound is out, silence and stillness are more silent and still.

Certain songs have rafted me through rough waters, helping me through the emotional stuff that a deteriorating physical condition throws up. They have been a factor in helping me to dialogue more honestly with myself and others. There have been times when I have sung the same song over and over again, sometimes with conscious understanding of the meaning, as with Sweet Honey's song 'I feel like going on, though trials mount on every side' (see p76), and sometimes just from feeling that the song is doing what is needed. Most of the time I sing just because I love singing.

About seven years ago, soon after my body had become unable to cope with the stress of trying to function as an able-bodied person, I was forced to review my life and reorganise it to take account of my physical limitations. Around the same time I also started using my voice in another way, having followed a whim and got a dog. Living with the boisterous young Charlie and trying to train him required a different vocal repertoire comprised of firmness, clarity of intention and some good shouting. Up till then I had not been in the habit of projecting my voice across the park. He also taught me to sing his way – head thrown back and howling!

I am convinced that these two extensions of the use of my voice played a part in empowering me to assert myself in my life again. At the same time I began to write poetry. One of the poems from that time was entitled 'No'. It went like this:

When the no is said
What next?

and when the no is said
I am no more drained dry
By their consumption

and when the no is said

in its many shapes, colours,
sounds and paces
dew *touches*
a tender shell
and life breathes in me

and when the no is said
I leap and bound along
the forest path

and they will have to find
another way
themselves

Using my voice has become so much part of me now that it has become quite difficult to define its role. I do know that life would be a lot harder if it was still trapped away inside me.

Linda Lawrence was faced with the death of a beloved child. In many past cultures, and still in some today, there were shared mourning rituals, a chance for relatives to give vent to their feelings. Linda's story tells of something we may all, at times, have felt we've lost.

I am not sure whether the experience helped to find expression for my grief, or if the profound effect connected more to the fact that, as a wheelchair-user, it was a way of expression that offered possibilities to open my mouth and use my voice in a way that held truth but no fear.

My eldest son, Adam, died two years before I came to the workshop. He was five years old. To try to explain that experience would be a book in itself. One thing I remember was the overwhelming desire to take myself to a hill or mountain, open my mouth and let out sounds that I have only heard in my head or in the animal world. Needless to say I swallowed all that sound for fear of appearing mad and got on with what felt like an alien way of dealing with something that was so present in my body, but had no space. In that grief was such anger and rage, mainly at a God I don't believe in (although I have always been in touch with a spiritual sense). I was also full of 'It's not fair.'

I am a wheelchair-user but I do not see myself as a victim on that account. It is part of who I am. My sense of identity has, obviously, been defined somewhat by this reality, in the same way that being a girl, then a woman, then a mother has combined to making me the woman I am, viewing the world the way I do. But, like the grief, I have had a sound in my head that expresses my deepest feelings of anger at the injustice, oppression, lack of equality and opportunity for education, work and creativity for wheelchair-users, for which spoken and written language never feels adequate.

And then I met Frankie at one of her voice workshops. Here at last was a space where I could learn a way of opening my mouth and making sounds that were a mixture of so many things. The sounds did not have to be pretty or make musical sense. They were real and full sounds that I recognised. That day I learnt how to open my mouth, throat and soul, releasing 'my voice' which, although it was my sound, had connections with the ancient history of women's suffering, joy and wisdom. I continue to use this technique for singing and when I have to talk in public and facilitate Disability Training Workshops, especially when the language of words does not seem enough. I just open my mouth and trust that somewhere inside is a connection to a world that is both individual and collective.

Stephanie Dowrick was faced with the possibility of her own death. She is a writer and psychotherapist, living in

Sydney. She wrote these words on Monday 9 December 1996, under the title 'Gospel'.

> Through many dangers, toils and snares,
> I have already come:
> 'Tis grace has brought me safe thus far
> And grace will lead me home.

The contribution below is made up from extracts of a piece written by Stephanie for a collection of essays by Amanda Lohrey under the title *Secrets*, published by Pan Macmillan, Australia. I thank Stephanie and Amanda for allowing me to reprint these extracts.

If I had a life to choose I would prefer to be a musician rather than a writer. Why? Because words are always limiting, aren't they? And because the contact with the audience is just so *immediate*, and because through music you're reaching to people's hearts in a *very* direct way. You transcend the self through the music, and you transcend the limitations between self and other through the music. There is not another art form that does it so powerfully.

The liberation of group singing for me is that it's an art form where I don't have to be the best, where my ego is not involved, where I don't have to be ever hoping for a solo, or to shine; where all I need to do is experience the music – experience the music rather than experience my ego through the music. That's the most amazing liberation.

I sang (gospel) in classes for five or six months before I went on a gospel tour of the US with Tony Backhouse. When I started I did feel somewhat embarrassed about being in a group of people I didn't know, doing something I felt very uncertain about, but I'd just had cancer and I thought, hell, you know, I'm just going to sing, because I might die and, I thought, my inhibitions are of no consequence here whatsoever.

Having cancer was the catalyst. It absolutely propelled me into music. I did a workshop with Frankie Armstrong when I had just come out of hospital, and somebody there told me that Tony Backhouse was giving classes. It was just the most enormous relief to be singing. And I was feeling very very stressed at the time – very stressed and distressed. I was parched: the music was like water.

What do people get from this? I can only speak for myself. I got, and get, a number of things. One is the opportunity to pray through music. It is, for me, a very intense and radiant form of meditation. When I sing, I really try to allow myself to recognise and experience that I'm singing in praise of loving God. Then there's also this amazing sense of being connected to other people – who may be complete strangers to you really – only through the music. I really like that. You can feel a kind of kinship of soul with people who, at the end of the class, just go off in their different directions. I like making connections that are not forged through words and discussion. And I feel very healed by the music. I felt that most particularly when we were travelling in the south singing every day. Singing every day and hearing great gospel music sung by others made the most *enormous* difference to me. I think it cured me of having cancer.

I haven't in my own therapy practice recommended singing to people as therapy. But last year when I was having this dreadful, dreadful time, I did some somatic (body-oriented) therapy. There were some days when I went to see my therapist when I was so depressed I could barely speak. And several times – he's a wonderful singer, this guy – several times he just stood up and started to sing. And I would force myself up, and I would also sing. I remember one memorable occasion when I couldn't speak, we were sitting in this complete kind of doldrum, and I stood up, and started to sing, and then he started to sing with me, and I moved myself out of the pits.

I think it's partly to do with your breathing; it's also partly posture, it's partly moving your mind, as you do in meditation, on to something very focused. But singing is more energetic than meditation often is. There's so much energy to it, and I think you can tune into a collective energy which reminds you that you are not alone. Of course, when you are depressed, that's when it's hardest to sing. But I had to – it was a *huge* act of will, a huge act of will to do it at all. It felt to me in some moments like a choice between life and death.

I will end this chapter with a short, moving story from last week. I was running a Voice Workshop in London and one of the participants came up to me at the end. 'Frankie, I was at a workshop you ran some dozen years ago. Do you remember teaching us a song called *Younda*?' Her mention of the song called to mind the haunting, gentle strains of this Hebridean lilt – a chant that was given to a woman by the seals. 'I sang it to my mother as she died. I held her hand and sang to her.' As Joan Mills has pointed out, this is to revive an ancient women's tradition of singing 'death croons' to the dying. I hope we all hear such beauty as our bodies move from being sieged to shuffling off this mortal coil.

Voices of Hope

Julie McNamara

My understanding of voice work is grounded within an appreciation of people as social beings, often alienated from our selves and becoming increasingly disconnected from our communities. My work is fired by a commitment to enabling people who have limited access to education or recreational facilities or to full participation in community life. I work with disenfranchised groups of people, often in troubled areas. For instance, I have worked in lock-in wards and other departments within a long-stay hospital, in mental health and in women's centres from Belfast to Bosnia. In this chapter I intend to focus on three projects, one in each of these settings, in order to show how voice work can activate people in distress in conflict situations.

The aim of my work is to create safe forums where people feel empowered to reclaim their voices. Through storytelling, they are given the opportunity to utter the unspeakable; and through songs of hope and songs of struggle as well as the use of non-verbal sound, to begin to play again with their own creativity. It is my belief that this work can start the journey to recovery and reconnection to a sense of community.

I trained as a drama therapist in the early eighties and then worked as an equal opportunities trainer for the GLC. As one of only two white women on a team of six, I learnt much about the dynamics of cultural difference and the hierarchies of power that we all engage in. When I moved on I was determined to use the skills I had learnt in group dynamics and the creative arts to work with marginalised groups – people without power, often segregated from their communities – who had little access to the arts. Throughout my work with each group, I discovered the importance of creating a forum where each person felt that her/his voice was heard. Each person's story was respected and valued. The learning that moved me into deeper work with voice was the immediacy of people's responses to music, to the vibrations of sound.

> Where there is gross injury, the soul flees...sometimes it drifts so far away it takes masterful propitiation to coax it back. A long time must pass before such a soul will trust enough to return...The retrieval requires several ingredients: naked honesty, stamina, tenderness, sweetness, ventilation of rage and humour. Combined, these make a song that calls the soul back home.
>
> *All in the End is Harvest*,
> Agnes Whitaker, editor

Our voices are the utterance of our souls in the world and a litmus of our spiritual and physical condition. Contrary to the thinking behind much of Western culture, we cannot split off our bodies from mind and spirit and remain whole and healthy. Nor can we separate ourselves from the cultural and social conditions in which we live. If we are at odds with the world, in emotional crisis or in political strife, our voices act as our barometers. Even when words fail us, our suffering is still conveyed in our voices. My use of voice work over these past 15 years has been about witnessing others' often unbearable pain through their struggle to find their own 'song that calls the soul back home'.

Before the process of normalisation (whatever that was intended to mean) and the decanting of the many big bins in mental healthcare in England, I worked in a long-stay institution for 'the mentally subnormal'. These terms were used even until the mid-1980s! 'Normalisation' and 'Community Care' then became the buzz words of a Tory government which viewed the chemically coshed inmates of these monstrous institutions as an economic liability. Working in such a place is a sore to the soul. The very walls are riddled with the vibrations of the lost and the lonely screaming out for salvation, for mother, for God, or whoever else had betrayed them. I was naive, I thought I could change things.

The hospital was a 2000-bed unit, a dark, forbidding place in beautiful surroundings, built in Hertfordshire during the Victorian era and governed with a characteristic cultural severity. I worked in the Social Education and Assessment Centre, lived in the nursing quarters and awoke each morning to the sound of one particular voice, counting monotonously each of the bricks around my window as she traced the mortar with her fingers. The days were filled with the dismal sounds of people in despair, some lost for ever in their torment. So, too, were the days filled with little joys and moments of magic that lent some meaning to the madness of choosing such a career path.

I will always hold on to the moment when Linda squeezed one of the nurse's hands and wouldn't let go, after all the staff in the voice and movement group that day had insisted she couldn't sing, wouldn't move and was a waste of a space in the circle! It was a startling moment for the staff member concerned and a turning point in Linda's life, for it contributed to her case being reassessed. She was subsequently moved to a higher grade ward and, little by little, was given back some modicum of choice over where and how she lived the rest of her life. Then there was Eddie, who was allowed out to negotiate the streets, learn about traffic and shops (and sometimes police stations, because he didn't always get it right). Eddie had been inside for 34 years for stealing a bicycle when he was nine years of age. Completely institutionalised, he went on trying to trade cigarette butts in spite of the fact that this salubrious estate ran its own shop within the grounds. Eddie loved to sing: he would shed tears when he sang 'for Ireland', as he put it – though he had never been to Ireland and as far as anybody knew had no connections there, except in his heart. He would often urge me to sing *The Wild Colonial Boy*, join in with gusto and then raise a hand authoritatively to indicate that he was taking over.

Each institution has its own way of doing things and sometimes magic comes in strange guises. I had persuaded Mary Francis, the senior in command, that we ought to have a women's group, bringing women together away from the wards. So it came about that, without knowledge of a single crochet, loop or knit and purl, I began running the 'Ladies' Knitting Workshop'. I was allowed to run a women's group, but only if the participants were producing something saleable, that could be construed as occupational therapy! We met every Wednesday for 12 months. We began in silence, or amid repetitive mutterings that seemed to have their own code. I would join the women for their knitting sessions and try to engage them in conversation. I would hum and the women would join me. Eventually we were singing together. Over the months that followed, slowly but surely, they opened up by talking and sharing their stories. I borrowed techniques from Reminiscence Theatre, which I had learned from Baz Kershaw and Gill Hadley, researching the songs and events of the thirties and forties, then talking about them and encouraging the women to tell their own versions of events. The women were very animated throughout this part of the session, but I must confess to my continuing aversion to one particular refrain. If I ever hear 'The Siegfreid Line' again it'll be the finish of me!

Each week I brought a song or a story to the circle and

each week I would wonder about Celie, in one corner of the room, who joined us religiously but sat in silence throughout. Celie was 54 years of age and had been hospitalised since she was a girl. She had been raped, and then abandoned by her family for 'bringing shame upon her mother's name', as her father had said when having her committed. Celie did not speak until spoken to. Then she only responded in clipped formulas: 'Yes, dear...No, dear...' or not at all. It was said that Celie had been an enquiring and creative woman in early adulthood, but the years of slave labour under the guise of occupational therapy seemed to have deadened her mind: stuffing cotton wool balls into plastic bags and other mindless tasks. I wondered about her continual attendance at the 'Knitting Circle' since she showed no interest in knitting. However, she seemed to enjoy the company, the music and general mayhem. She was obviously a great listener on the quiet.

After three months or so of storytelling and voice work in this miserable context, I began to despair. The women loved to tell their stories. Everybody enjoyed the songs and the banter. But we were going round and round the same pattern like hamsters in a wheel, forever caged together. I questioned my own integrity, working within a system that I fundamentally disapproved of. I felt I was perpetuating this culture of deprivation that incarcerated troubled souls. I felt tormented with questions. What was my role here? Was this institution our imaginative and intelligent response to disabled people, to people in distress? Was this to be my only contribution to their emotionally impoverished lives?

Gradually I got on to a different tack. I began to encourage the women to use our time together, their stories and their voice work, to role rehearse each woman's case conference. People in this institution were rarely offered access to Mental Health Review Tribunals at that time, so there was nobody speaking in their corner or representing them at all on the ward rounds or at the infrequent case reviews. These were all vulnerable women who had been patients for many years. They were women who had been diagnosed by the medical profession as 'morally degenerate' – for 'promiscuity' or for giving birth to children out of wedlock – in the 1930s and 1940s. Effectively they had been tried without jury and incarcerated with little or no explanation. While these women were abandoned in this institution, they were being denied full citizenship and basic human rights. The seniors at the hospital seemed to believe that most of these women were so 'institutionalised' they would never survive beyond the hospital gates. They were rarely given an opportunity to speak to the authorities, let alone the chance to offer an opinion. Many of them would not feel confident enough, faced with a panel of doctors, to account for themselves and represent their own wishes and requirements at a case review meeting.

Together we rehearsed the possibilities, through role plays, self-assertion techniques and a great deal of singing. Each time the women told their stories and expressed their dreams and fantasies, they grew closer to creating the reality to which they aspired.

During the last six months of my employment at the hospital I became distracted with my own struggle, having begun to realise how institutionalised I was becoming myself. Then, one day at the Ladies' Knitting Workshop, Celie spoke. I was pottering about with old knitting patterns that we rarely used as some of the women were incredibly creative with wool. I suddenly became aware of Celie staring at me. She was intensely focused. As usual, the room smelt of anxiety and old nicotine. The other women's chattering began to hush. Celie's focus had cut through the chemical cosh that was the order of the day. Suddenly her voice emerged, bold and vibrant. In a steady, certain tone, she said: 'Get me out of here. I don't belong in here. I want out!'

It took Celie almost two years to convince the hospital authorities that she could survive life in the community outside. There were many setbacks en route. Before I left the group and the hospital behind me, I witnessed Celie and the other women using the knitting workshop to imagine their future lives and fantasise about their freedom. It is only by imagining the possibilities that we can begin to create the reality. Many of those last sessions together were like singing at a wake. The women mourned their lost years and partied at the thought of life ahead. Hopes were raised and dashed many times. Afterwards I kept in touch. Celie was finally released with three other women who had given birth to children in the hospital back in the late 1930s. They were a group of firm friends, committed to each other. They went on living together, not too far away from the hospital they'd known all of their lives. As for me, on the day I left my job I joined a team of creative therapists to set up a centre for personal development holidays on Skyros Island, Greece – moving from the sublime to the ridiculous, or vice versa. I have remained a member of that team for some 16 summers now.

After my work at the hospital, I thought a lot about the importance of songs in community, of voices in the open, of stories that must be told. In examining my own input and motivation during that time, I went back to my own story, to my roots in Ireland. During the mid-1980s, I spent a lot of my time retracing the songs and stories that had meant so much to me in my childhood. Call it synchronicity or just a happy accident, I was then invited by Marie MulHolland to work in the North of Ireland. I went to Belfast and Derry to perform as a singer and to run workshops. Marie was later to become part of the European Women's Network in the six counties. The network was a committee of 10 women's groups which worked across sectarian divides, committed to restoring peace in Ireland. They were Protestants, Catholics, Quakers and pacifists of no definable religion. These were the courageous women who eventually persuaded Mary Robinson, the first president elect in 300 years, to set foot in the six counties. It was these inspirational women, working tirelessly behind the scenes, who truly began the peace process – and I had the good fortune to meet and work with them.

It was August 1989. The first extradition from Dublin into Belfast had just taken place and the streets were filled with unrest. Six bombs had gone off in the city centre. The skies were full of the sounds of sniper fire. My workshop had had to be postponed, as the building was so close to where one of the bombs had gone off. Later that evening I was nervous as I went off to perform a concert at Madden's Bar in Smithfields, Belfast. I set off with Judy Coutinho, a magnificent guitarist I was touring with, thinking that nobody would show up tonight of all nights. What I met there challenged all of my fantasies about communities living with the backdrop of imperialism and conflict. Arriving at the venue, I was moved to find the place jam packed full of women from every community. There were women from the Falls, women from the Shankhill, the Divis flats and from both ends of Murder Mile. I expressed my gratitude at such a turn-out and was told in no uncertain terms: 'Let the boys have their war! Our business is building bridges . . . '

Marie reminded me that James Connolly himself had advised the defeated striking women from the Belfast mill in the early 1900s 'When you go back in, go in singing!' That was the spirit in which the audience had arrived that night and I will never forget it. I have to smile as I think of the irony of the title of our show that night – *Rebel Without a Clue!*

After the concert I was inspired when a group of the women, reflecting on the war, talked of the bonds across their divided communities and the importance of working together for change. It was dangerous ground to tread, but each of the women there was determined to find peace in *her* lifetime. At one point, agreeing to set aside the old unionist arguments, the women sang together an old miners' union song:

Step by step the longest march can be won, can be won
Many stones do build an arch singly none, singly none
And by union what we will can be accomplished still
Drops of water turn a mill singly none, singly none.[1]

That night, in true Irish style, we had the obligatory 'lock in'. Most of the population of the bar remained to drink and sing. I watched a group of women from Maguires Bridge in Fermanagh singing together in the traditional way, gathered around the main voice, holding her hands and supporting her back, swaying with her and calling the song forth. There was such a supportive tenderness and physical intimacy in their singing. I have taken that style of singing into my voice workshops and now work in a much more physical way, encouraging people to bring the song forth. I have the women of Fermanagh to thank for that learning.

In July 1997 my partner, based in Sarajevo, invited me to work with a women's centre in Tuzla, Bosnia, to provide drama therapy training, music and voicework. I was asked to train educational psychologists, former primary school teachers and fieldworkers from the collective centres. All of these were women working with traumatised children from rural areas, now living in temporary accommodation. After Srebrenica was annihilated, centres were created to house displaced persons. These 'collective centres' are based in municipal buildings, schools and factories where hundreds of women and children have been temporarily housed after being driven from their homes. Their lives are bleak, with little or no provision for adult education, schooling or recreation. The women attending the training I provided are committed to restoring equilibrium to their country, to educating the children and encouraging hope.

Most of the surviving children who were witness to horrific atrocities in the war have behavioural problems. For them, violence has been their most enduring experience of the world. For many of the adults too, life in these last seven years has been about surviving the traumas of war. If they were not directly involved as victims of atrocities, many of the Bosnian professionals I trained were experiencing secondary traumatisation, as they had had to hear first hand, over and over again, the terrible stories of those who had survived.

I travelled to Bosnia with some trepidation, having read and heard the stories of survivors of the rape camps. I was expecting to find some deeply disturbed people, spiritually crushed and merely hanging on to life. As we journeyed from the heart of Sarajevo into the Biser women's centre in Tuzla we passed through incredibly beautiful scenes of breath-taking landscape, but then through sudden images of devastation as we passed by the remains of community life in rural Bosnia which had been almost entirely erased. I could not find a single house unscathed by the impact of bloody-minded hatred. Villages were completely gutted, buildings decimated and only fragile reminders of human existence remained – an overturned pram in a garden, a table still standing in the ravages of a derelict house, walls shattered from shell fire and shrapnel. I could not abate my tears and wept silently for most of that journey.

Not surprisingly, the population of large areas of Bosnia are suffering from Traumatic Stress Syndrome. I expected that. I knew it was going to be intense work, but I was not ready for the immediacy of their responses, for the vibrancy and sheer joy. I had felt daunted by the task ahead, thinking of the thousands of women silenced by the trauma of repeated rapes. But this particular group of women were intent on creativity. They were dynamic women full of laughter, mischief and song! Their courage and determination to re-build their communities, and to move beyond mere survival and thrive, is a powerful message to us all.

So we came together to play, create and restore song to silenced voices. And each of the women involved was determined to give voice to the disempowered, to those disenfranchised individuals who had become too traumatised to speak, let alone tell their stories. The women in the group were Zlatter, Asima, Ader, Jasmina, Nasiha, Esmina, Mira and our translator Gabi, all professionals working with the traumatic disorders of their colleagues and clients, within their dislocated communities. We worked in rhythm and voice, soothing and cajoling each other, re-discovering the joys of making music together. We worked with our whole bodies using sound vibration, playing off the walls and the ceiling of the building.

From the sparsest resources (plastic bottles and hard-paper carrier bags) we constructed percussion instruments to join the swelling chorus. We started with simple mesmeric rhythms and added field songs, vocal calls that would be familiar to Bosnian children from the rural communities. I taught them some Gambian work songs, simple call and response hollers, that carried across the village while we worked. Our voices resounded throughout those buildings, bringing a new vibration to replace the rattle of the gun. Voices of jubilation were replacing the paralysing sounds of destruction. I was deeply moved by the experience of working with the women of Tuzla and I felt heartened, knowing that they would go on to share their discoveries with hundreds of others in their fields of work.

International aid in Bosnia has concentrated on the

complex problem of rehousing displaced persons and supporting rebuilding programmes. The focus has been on basic human needs, food and shelter. From as early as 1992, during the intensity of the conflict, some international organisations were providing psychosocial programmes supporting women and children traumatised by the war. Those programmes have slowed down to a trickle, but for many people the symptoms of trauma are only just emerging as areas previously torn apart by the conflict are restored to relative safety.

Music as therapy has been, and continues to be, a solid part of the post-conflict rehabilitation and cultural reconstruction in the former Yugoslavia. Mostar, in Bosnia, is the site of one of the finest music therapy centres in Europe, funded by Pavarotti and validated by the Faculties of Medicine and Music at the University of Sarajevo. I went back to Bosnia in October and was inspired by the signs of rebuilding, the sheer optimism on the streets of Sarajevo and a sense that the sap is rising again.

In looking back over the work I have been involved in, I grow ever more convinced of the power of our voices – whether those voices are breathing life into our stories or breathing through the wounds with which we live. I am certain of the healing power of the human voice – of non verbal sound, or singing – for the individual voice in isolation or in the crowd. In whatever context we are living out our lives, we each need to find our own ingredients for the 'song that calls the soul back home'!

Notes

1 An American poem for the National Miners' Union, set to the slightly adapted tune 'O the praties they grow small' by Ysaye Barnwell for Sweet Honey in the Rock.

Bibliography

McNamara, Julie, 'Out of Order – Madness is a Feminist and Disability Issue', in *Encounters with Strangers – Feminism and Disability*, The Women's Press, London, 1996

—with Jeanette Copperman, 'Institutional Abuse in Mental Health Settings', *Institutional Abuse*, Routledge, London, 1999.

—'Singing in Tuzla', *Women in Music* (January 1997)

—'Post Trauma Drama', *Mental Health Care* (October 1999)

Julie McNamara writes a monthly column for DIAL magazine and has had poetry published by the Survivors Press.

Favourite books

Blood-Patterson, Peter, ed, *Rise Up Singing*, Sing Out Publication, Bethlehem, Pennsylvania, 1992

Huntingdon, Gale, ed, *Sam Henry's Song of the People*, University of Chicago Press, Athens, 1990

Sachs, Oliver, *Seeing Voices*, Picador, London, 1990

Powerspeak
Women and Their Voices in the Workplace

Patsy Rodenburg

Earlier this year I was asked to conduct a series of voice workshops for one of the most influential companies on the planet; a company that profoundly affects all levels of industry and management skills in Western business.

I was briefed by the directors of the company. By employing me they were admitting that they had a huge problem at the heart of their company, a problem that was costing them millions of dollars a year. It existed among the high fliers. The creative blood of the company. These young executives were constantly alienating colleagues and business associates through insensitive and arrogant use of voice and language. In communicating, they came over as dismissive of others. In the words of their directors, they were 'pompous, supercilious and too powerful'. My job was to humanise their communication skills and encourage sensitivity. My initial reaction was, is this a new problem? No, it wasn't. The company had always employed the brightest and most dynamic of graduates. What the company had suddenly recognised was that in the industrial climate of the late twentieth century, these qualities were not appreciated or tolerated. They had identified a trend towards transformation of practices and were determined to keep ahead of the game.

My first workshop demonstrated a clear example of the problem and gave me a startling insight into a new business consciousness. I had 19 young, dynamic men and one, seemingly reserved, woman. I started the workshop with exercises to encourage listening, the unthreatening use of the body and voice, the sensitive use of language and the power of words. They were bright and understood the work but found the physical and breath work difficult. As anyone in the voice field knows, if you can connect fully to your body, breath and voice, you have a chance to connect to your emotions and through the emotions you can become sensitised to the rest of the world. This was a new experience and for some of them very disturbing. They were feeling vulnerable. One of them commented, 'We are really just brains on sticks'.

As the workshop progressed, I worked on each participant individually. Their fears grew. The last person to work – which is often the case – was the young woman. As she got up, to my horror there was an immediate unwholesome energy in the room. An energy thrown at this woman by most of the group that was partly sexual intimidation, partly mocking, with a pinch of the schoolboy wolf whistle. No wonder she was reserved. I was shocked but had come across similar situations in other workplaces. I stopped the session and called them to order. They squirmed and apologised to her. Privately, I wondered whether she was the butt of their fear, or had she in their history encouraged their behaviour by flirting to aid their acceptance of her female presence in a very male world, or was she not very good at her job?

The last was proved wrong immediately. She started her presentation. She was good; better than any of them. She did need work on her voice – it was underpowered – but what she was doing was very effective. She was open, clear and uncluttered, approachable, sensitive, listening. Nothing in her work got in the way. Any tension that covers our voice or words is, in some way, off-putting. She had no off-putting habits. All the men had tried to bluff their way through their presentations. Bluff is common in male habits of voice. Bluff: being too loud; refusing to be interrupted or respond to the energy of a group; making general eye contact or looking down on the auditors. Pinning the audience to their seats and not tolerating interaction, keeping attention and control by brute force. For many years this form of delivery was common and it was considered effective. In fact it was taught as the way to control your employees.

All this flashed through my mind and with these thoughts the light began to dawn. The woman's skills were the ones I had been employed to teach the men. The wheel had come full circle; the times are changing. Business is now needing and is prepared to invest in teaching men what have until now been seen as traditionally female vocal habits and skills.

This article is an attempt to chart the journey I have made over the last 25 years with hundreds of women trying to succeed and survive in the workplace, a workplace that was initially completely male, where the female skills were undervalued. This article is only based on experience and work. I am not qualified to comment in any academic way. I have not spent years researching the topic of women in the workplace. I've merely worked with women striving within it. I can only describe the journey and the comments and observations made by women tackling their problems practically on a daily basis.

To be completely honest, when I entered the voice world in the seventies I only expected to work with performers. This expectation was quickly shattered. By the mid-seventies, I was constantly working with lay men and women. I was teaching in prisons. I was teaching teachers, lawyers, bankers, politicians and business people. And I was being approached weekly to work with women struggling to establish themselves in the workplace. The common cry was that their voice, presentation and interview skills, their language, failed them in their careers, in interviews, in controlling others and later, after promotion, it failed them in the boardroom.

The voice might be only the tip of the iceberg, but it was one that mattered and it matters today. I journeyed into this work without any knowledge of how it would develop. I just started to solve problems. People started to come for help in these areas in the seventies as a last resort. The work is now more known and appreciated, and consequently it gets done earlier. But at that time it was about working in crisis.

This crisis helped me to formalise my philosophy of voice. I began to passionately believe that we are all born with a great voice, a clear, free and natural voice. This idea grew as simple voice work revealed wonderful voices overwhelmed by dire vocal problems. The first batch of professional women who arrived generally hated their sound or, more accurately, had been taught to believe that their voice was inadequate. These negative reflections had created physical clutter in the body, breath and voice that ultimately constricted their free voice. Life batters the joy of voice out of many people and these were the people who sought help. Of course this is a simple explanation, but whatever the cause of our voices being restricted – and there are many, since every voice is unique – somewhere along the line the physical result is lodged and manifested in the body, the breath and the voice itself. A lost voice is lost power, and voice work, therefore, often empowers the speaker.

It seems that after the initial intellectual awareness of the feminist movement, the physical manifestations surfaced in the mid-seventies. Women seeking my help either felt that their voices were denied, not heard or, if they had good strong voices, they were mocked or called unfeminine, their vocal power deemed inappropriate.

In the workplace women felt tolerated as servers but not as equals or leaders – in those positions they weren't tolerated. In the arenas of power men didn't want to hear women holding or expressing opinions. Gossiping, giggling and flirting yes, but an intelligent woman speaking with freedom, clarity and power was too much and these women were constantly punished. In hindsight, no wonder voice specialists were sought by professional women.

This story really starts or at least was clarified in the theatre. In the seventies it started to become fashionable for actresses to play male roles and so at this time I also had many requests for this kind of transformation. At first the actresses and I believed that to appear male you had merely to lower the voice. A lower pitch would indicate maleness.

This idea was rapidly scuppered. A lower voice was only a cosmetic change that didn't really communicate maleness. As I worked on this problem, I began to realise the signals communicating maleness were connected to every physical aspect of power and a person's relationship to power. This power is expressed throughout the body, breath, voice, speech and use of language. Every stage of communication expresses power or its denial. In the actresses' case language wasn't an issue as they had a male text, but the rest was essential to any truthful transformation.

Simple shifts throughout the whole voice system, energy and focus could effectively communicate a man. These shifts were small in technical terms but huge in emotional ones. Panic set in with these shifts as they made the women feel sensations of power and control to which they felt they had no right. To appear male they had to stand, walk, sit, breathe, look and listen differently – all these shifts of habit before uttering a sound. I started to categorise these differences and habits. Remember this list is general: no one fits neatly into any category.

Male communication habits revolve around taking up space. Not giving in. Standing feet apart, sitting legs open. Chest open or puffed out. Energy forward, probing. Head held high. Choosing to look or not look without apology. Breathing slowly and deeply into the body. Speaking when they want to and not rushing. Driving the voice. Often being too pushy without apology. Not falling off a line, but sustaining an idea. Speaking about what they want to talk about and not being distracted or feeling the necessity to change subject matter if asked. Listening without supporting another speaker. Not withdrawing when challenged or interrupted, in fact just getting louder to drown out any interference. Clear, sure and uncompromising language. Words without room for debate.

If we take these habits to the highest level of confidence and self-satisfaction, you can witness a speaker pausing – long pauses without the fear of being interrupted – droning on without realising or perhaps even caring that they are boring the listener rigid. Speaking about things the listener has no idea of and perhaps relating everything in personal anecdotes.

This list highlights the most extreme of the male bluff techniques. Of course it is out of balance and later I will be describing the work that puts both male and female habits into harmony. Truly powerful people don't have to bluff; they can be still and quiet. But 25 years ago, these habits seemed vivid and lodged within the male domain and maybe became more exaggerated when challenged by powerful women.

Female habits revolve around reduction, denial, giving way and not taking up space.

Standing, sitting with feet together, thighs clamped, spine slightly slumped, shoulders rounded, chest collapsed. Head looking down. Physically apologising or being demure. Short, high, rushed breath. Never taking a full breath because that would be taking full power and space. Speaking when not ready. Hesitating and struggling to get into a conversation. Backing down if confronted. Losing steam and falling off lines. Changing topics of conversation if the listener seemed uninterested in what was being discussed. Rushing into incoherence. Being off voice. Too quiet, too high pitched, not showing passion in the voice but being a good listener by supporting other speakers with encouraging sounds and remarks. The most extended form of these habits could include whining, a very effective means for an underdog to get her way – you give in to stop the noise and the nagging. Chipping away at the resistance of the powerful member of a partnership. As a last resort, screeching.

These habits were the antithesis of the male domain. They were the habits of victims and were in greatest emphasis in cross gender communications, particularly in the presence of an aggressive man. Women talking to women could be freed from some of these habits, but they were very entrenched in most women in the seventies.

These descriptions of male and female habits could be interpreted as energy, and the qualities of male and female energy can be found mixed within each individual and sex.

The immediate result of this work was that women, by adapting the more extreme male habits, could appear male organically. The transformation in theatre started to be deep and filled, not a caricature male voice but a male being. This work made me assess all my work differently. I began to notice how hard it was for my female students to engage in open discussions with men in class. Even if there were only 3 men in a group of 20, the women were the last to come forward and contribute to a discussion and the first to give way. All the listed habits were manifest and even if I worked openly on these habits they were so physically entrenched that they were hard to let go. I realised by the late seventies that women had a huge mountain to climb. It was no good just recognising the problems intellectually; they had to be worked out as these physical habits were constantly letting them down and were communicating weakness subliminally in every act of expression. It starts the moment you are seen. If the chairwoman of a board didn't enter a space and sit with all the habits of power, however good her voice or language, she would fail on some levels. However good the female politician was in her constituency, if she stood weakly to ask a question in the House of Commons no one would listen or even see she was there.

It occurred to me that we gather habits in order to survive. We might not like the habit or it becomes redundant and has to be dug out of us, but it is there for a reason. At some stage we need it to defend ourselves or manipulate others. If we let a habit go we will lose some of the benefits. Three weeks ago I had a young female student confide in me – this story is typical and versions of it crop up weekly.

This student has many of the female victim habits. Closed body that fidgets and wriggles when she speaks, high gasped breath and a very 'off' voice with no support, no energy. She has been working hard and has begun to achieve physical and vocal power. What she confided was a wonderful example. 'When I use my full voice Daddy doesn't give me money.' She has learnt that the £50 handouts come only when she is using, in her words, her 'sweet voice'.

But in the workplace women's 'sweet voices' weren't being rewarded. Flirting, being sweet and silly often made life easier, but these habits did not facilitate promotion. And there began to appear a bigger sting in the tail. Many women, by using their good female habits of listening, reassuring, giving way and stroking, were irreplaceable in the lower levels of a company. The really good PA or personnel manager was never going to get a promotion, however well she interviewed, because she was so successful in serving the higher status men and men couldn't, and didn't want to, do her work. If she was in a company that did have the grace to promote her, she found herself in a position whereby all the habits that made her good at her job – ie supporting others – were redundant on the board or as a manager. My response to all these problems (and I describe the work below) is to train the whole voice so any speaker can move appropriately around the whole gamut of habits. Starting from the centre of every voice, you can develop enough awareness to choose your habit. Express power or passiveness.

So the theatrical work informed the work I was doing with professional women. Many of these women believed that if they lowered the pitch of their voice, pushed it down and constricted it they would achieve power and be on an equal footing with men in the workplace. After all, that is what Mrs Thatcher did as we moved into the eighties.

I resisted this option as I sensed that, like the work with actresses, this would only produce a cosmetic result. Instead I started to teach these women all the discoveries I had made in the theatre work. I tried to balance the positive aspects of each group of habits – marrying the good qualities of each. We worked on taking physical space, finding a stillness in the body. Breathing low and fully without rushing. Good strong breath support, accessible when needed. Strong eye contact. A full, strong, sustained and focused voice. Speech without hesitation or irrelevant words or sounds – 'um's' and 'ah's'. Held lines, no falling off. Listening without losing sight of what you want to say. Keeping to a point until it has been fully addressed.

The feedback on this work was good; it was not only helping many women to understand their own voices and habits but started to inform them of their male colleagues' habits. This put some women at an advantage. Some were rapidly promoted. Many reported much more efficient performances at interviews, board meetings and debates. They felt they were in greater control of themselves and their colleagues. A very common observation was that male colleagues were more tolerant of one another – they would allow each other to ramble on – but would dismiss a woman if she did this. At least with knowledge, women could identify the behaviour and act accordingly.

Women also started to recognise that the arenas of power jarred female energy. The actual geography of the House of Commons, the Stock Exchange and lecture halls was designed for conflict. To exist in these spaces women had to face an energy that was intentionally aggressive – an energy that many women organically fear and withdraw from, but that most men adore. They had to draw themselves together and engage on a very different level.

One female MP defined this challenge as the formal versus the informal. She realised that women were better communicators in the informal – one to one or sitting in a circle with no formal leader. Men thrived in the formal. She also referred to the formal as the feudal!

In geographical terms there were certain danger zones. Conducting business in bars with alcohol could send the wrong messages to men. In the seventies and early eighties, it was still conventional for men to stand in a pub while women sat – thus excluding the women from the action. Men did a great deal of business in pubs and bars, so women had to change the attitude of men within a bar or change the place where business was done. Office parties or conferences are still great arenas for men to safely talk business, but not so for women. Even last year a female bank manager said she had never been allowed to do business in a bar without some male colleague coming on to her. We had this discussion at a conference after I had done a workshop. During the discussion, which was in a hotel bar, two male participants of the conference then tried to intervene and pick us up. Both of us were soberly dressed and neither of us was flirting!

Having mentioned flirting, I have to say no serious high flier ever risks this at work. Some women admit that they have tried, but it has always backfired. Most miss flirting as it has, historically, been a great aid in bridging difficult moments in a male/female dialogue – we've all tried to flirt with the police officer who has stopped us for speeding – but use it in the wrong context and you are in trouble. Many women resent always having to be too efficient and grown up. The little helpless girl voice has also been a good ploy in the past when in need of help or just overwhelmed. Women in power always report there is no relaxation or respite on their journey to power and then on the one to keep it. A top saleswoman said recently, 'I can never afford to have too much to drink as it would be circulated around the office the next day with everything I said reported. My male colleagues can be rolling in the gutter without comment'.

As women achieved more commanding presentation skills they had to face the next challenge – language. To keep up with the men some women started to swear – yet this often made them shunned even more. Others said they tried to tell jokes – not a very usual activity for women. Joke telling is a great male bonding activity and again is a useful faucet into business deals. Only a few women said they could do this – most failed and felt foolish trying.

One powerful chairwoman of a multi-national company worked with me and soon found she could control the boardroom and command a great deal of respect. However, when there was a coffee break the men resorted to talking about football, a subject she knew nothing about. This effectively kept her out. Ever resourceful, she studied matches and teams. To her horror, when she joined in with football remarks, they deftly changed the subject to rugby.

Although the concept of political correctness in language is good, initially it opened up a lot of women to ridicule. Their language rights were simply mocked (although that seemed to calm down a bit in the late nineties).

It was also clear in the eighties that successful women not only had to change their physique, voice and language but they had to change their thought structures. They had to structure thought more directly and not be so lateral and emotional in their thinking. Objective not subjective. The adverse side of this change led to many who achieved it being called 'hard'. It was this accusation of hardness that began to trouble many women in the late eighties and into the nineties.

I started to notice a different temperature in workshops. I began to receive requests from women to have workshops in humanising their skills. The women in these workshops were highly skilled and successful communicators in their fields but they were beginning to resent having to adopt male habits – after all, many were mothers and needed their natural nurturing skills at home, so why not at work! They were becoming aware that their whole relationship to language, thought and feeling was different from men and that they didn't want to change their nature – although ironically they all had, to some extent, used the male habits to obtain power! Some recognised this and felt ashamed that they had used some of the worst habits learnt from men, bullying other women and victimising men in lower positions while using the worst habits of women – flirting inappropriately with men in higher positions.

Something had been lost. Women felt empty and hollow. They were losing the skills that have always made life interesting for women, the skills that in some cases had put them in power in the first place. The skills of listening, supporting, sharing emotional experience with others, bringing out the best in work mates. Allowing others to contribute and express themselves in a shared experience, not a lecture. Enjoying human communication and emotional intelligence, not always being a rational control freak. As one woman said to me, 'I'm in danger of losing my grace'.

An older and very wise politician summed it up with an equation relating to her career. She was a good debater (male trait) plus a great listener (female trait) which made her presence more palatable to male politicians and therefore equalled power. But she was old enough to have invested in all those female skills before honing her male ones – which she maintains are absolutely necessary if you wish to keep power. Her real concern is that her younger colleagues are a generation of women who are just using male habits. They have not lived through a time when female habits were lauded and therefore they have not invested in them. They are in danger of losing a connection to their female energy and if they do, something might break within them. Around conferences and workshops I've posited this opinion and have had only positive feedback in as much as the younger women are relieved that they can allow themselves to be less aggressive and more passive when appropriate.

This is still in debate. But if I return to the story at the beginning of the article, men are already striving to learn the female habits and in some cases women will also have to relearn them alongside their hard-fought for and found male ones. It might sound as if I only work with women. In fact I've worked with men as much if not more. The men who came for work in the seventies and eighties needed exactly the same skills as the women. They were men who needed more power in their voices. However, in the nineties I started to see many more men who were considered too powerful, too bossy or even a bully in the workplace. Their company was investing money for them to learn the female habits of listening and giving way.

So where does this all leave the work? Let's return to theatre and the basic training actors receive. The physical, vocal, speech listening and language demands made on an actor are immense. They are trained to be flexible, to work as a group, and they have to be heard clearly in a variety of venues. They must be able to make many forms of thought, feeling and language real. They must move easily between the formal and informal. No wonder actors are now being used at every level of business and industry to train employees!

Most training starts from the concept of centre. The middle way. A balance between male and female energy. A place of absolute strength and absolute vulnerability. The natural breath and voice are freed. All habits, male or female, are cleaned out of the system. The voice is stretched and placed forward so that words can be effortlessly released. The speech muscles are worked to facilitate clear speech. Listening is taught. Not only the ability to hear better but the ability to listen without prejudice. Use of language is exercised. Different styles of language, thought structure and intensity are explored. All this work enables an actor to transform, to change voice, walk, language, thought and feeling, etc. It is a starting point of harmony which can move when appropriate to any place of energy.

The finished place towards which all this is leading is often termed 'being in the moment'. It is the start and the end of the work. A marriage between all energy. All being possible, all being right and all energy depending on all other forms of energy. This might sound mystical but the work is completely practical and it is this work I now do with men and women in business. Transformation is possible. No difference is wrong. Power when appropriate and vulnerability when needed. To recognise fear in yourself and have compassion for it in others.

To have choice
To have strength
To have grace.

Releasing the Spirit
The Voice in Self-defence

Annie Neligan

I was on holiday, walking along in a bit of a dream. Suddenly someone leapt on me from behind. I just froze. I couldn't remember any of the self-defence moves you'd taught us, but I did remember the most important thing – that I could do *something*. I just turned around and *roared* in his face! He jerked back, let go of me and ran off.

Chris was telling me about an attack experienced years after coming to a self-defence course. As so often when we defend ourselves successfully, it was her voice that came to the rescue, that poured out her indignation, her anger and her conviction in her own right to look after herself and that overwhelmed her attacker.

After years of teaching self-defence to women I am still amazed at the power of our voices. Women attend these courses for all sorts of reasons, but each hoping to find, in some way they can't imagine, a confidence that will transform her from feeling like a victim in the face of anything from harassment to violence. Among the range of skills we encourage women to develop – which include becoming grounded, use of our senses and intuition, assertive body language and physical techniques learnt from martial arts – the voice is a crucial key to unlocking that source of power.

First, I'll give you an idea why I teach self-defence to women. I work from the premise that women live much of our lives controlled more or less by the anticipation of aggression or violence from men on the street, at work, in our homes. I believe that, while our only ultimate safety lies in working to change societies which tolerate and condone violence towards women and children, we can also work as individual women to increase our own sense of power and safety. On our courses at the National Women's Self-Defence Teachers Association we teach women ways of defending themselves from specific violent assaults, but our emphasis is more on changing the state of mind in which fear of such assaults can keep us.

Learning physical techniques, adapted to different abilities, is integral to rebuilding a sense of confidence and trust in our bodies. Even more important, however, is building confidence in our right to defend ourselves and in our inner strength and existing skills. Most of us have to free ourselves from the learnt beliefs that as women we are weaker than men, potential victims, deserving of the violence we experience or responsible for it. So we have to change our attitudes, rebuild that early but vanished belief in our own resources, before any physical response will be effective.

Crucial to this process is our belief that women will develop most confidence in classes taught by women. Men as tutors will help to perpetuate the idea that *they* are the ones with the greatest skill and strength, which we must try to imitate. Women learning from men are inhibited from using their experience, expressing their fears and developing alternative sources of strength.

So what do we do in our sessions?
We look at:
- how we can balance ourselves, stand strongly, drawing up power from the ground
- how we can give out messages of sureness in the way we hold our bodies, messages about our right to our space
- how we use our faces, particularly our eyes, to

express our determination not to accept invasion
- how we can use our senses to anticipate threats, to negotiate them, deflect them
- how we can develop a whole range of strengths that are nothing to do with traditional male muscular force
- how we can learn to move from the pelvis, using principles from a range of martial arts
- how we can focus our energy on the weak points of an aggressor, whether those are in his body or his ego!

And central to all these we use voice. This may consist of practising the firm statement and restatement of what we want and don't want. It may be learning to yell boldly, at full throttle. We practise breathing deeply, loosening chests and throats. We do exercises where we find out how, by adding our voices to a push, a strike, or a kick, we increase both our confidence and our effectiveness.

Try it for yourself. Thump your fist into a cushion. Then breathe out forcefully as you thump. Then, thump again, shouting 'Ha' from deep in your chest. Register how your feelings change with each of the blows.

We work to change where our voices come from, our chest not our throat, our belly not our head, learning that a scream can hurt us and stick in our throat, whereas a shout comes from somewhere much deeper and surer. We see how quietly challenging someone who is intimidating us, asking what he's up to at just the right moment, can throw his guard, rock his complacent sense of power and give us the advantage we need.

Ask a friend to approach you from behind. As they draw near, turn and face them. Say firmly: 'What do you want?' See how they respond.

*

Lots of women find our first sessions using voice really difficult. We can feel so vulnerable, so exposed, when first using our voices loudly. We practise in pairs and in groups, so that women can gain confidence in the well of sound. We discover what an amazing sense of power we can experience in a huge collective roar.

So now, having watched women learning the power of the voice for so long that I almost take it for granted, I would like to explore two questions: one, Why are our voices such a powerful instrument in self-defence? two, Why is it so difficult for us to tap into this source of power? These two questions are intricately intertwined and I haven't attempted here to separate them out. Instead, I look at the immediate effects of using our voices in self-defence situations. I then explore some of the deeper messages that we and others associate with our voices and the implications of these for how we look after ourselves.

Our voices release our breath. Women are often worried that in a scary situation they will panic and freeze. We may freeze, hold our breath in which case the fright squeezes our voices out of existence. But our system is flooding with adrenaline, ready for action. Our voices will get our breathing going again, whether it's to ask someone what they are up to or to roar full in their faces. Our voices can act as the crucial switch from holding in, feeling overwhelmed by fear, to an outward projection of our determination to defend ourselves.

Our voices help us express the movement from inward-directed fear to outward-directed anger, help us become an exploding ball of rage which can turn the tables on an aggressor. The message is not only to him, but to ourselves. As one woman said, exhilarated by her first punches, 'When I shout I feel strong!'

Our voices convince not only our assailant but also ourselves of our determination. The act of shouting in a frightening situation signifies, both to us and the world, that we are taking action, moving out of passivity. It's not the noise by itself that is the point. I don't have much faith in mugger alarms: not only can they be tricky to use, but they encourage the idea that what we most need to do is appeal for help. Shouting is not just about attracting attention. What is more important as we shout is the message to the assailant of who he has to reckon with.

Nor is the volume of our voice what's most important: it's the quality of the sound, the energy in it. Think how a kitten in a confrontation with a huge dog can make it back off with the determination injected into a *hissss*! And it's not the words that matter. I saw an elderly Asian woman being harassed on the street by English children: she saw them off in Bengali. It was the tone of her voice that convinced them she meant business.

Our voices serve to focus our power. Martial artists use this shout and call it a '*Kee ai*'. Tennis players shout on a fast serve, lumberjacks as they chop into a stubborn tree trunk.

Try it. Stand in an easy relaxed stance. Punch an imaginary solar plexus in front of you. Do it again more powerfully. Now focus not only your fist but your voice on that target and punch again with a shout – any word will do. You are focusing your eyes, your voice, your physical power, your determination, all on one point. Feel the difference.

As our eyes are the windows to our souls so, I believe, are our voices to our source of power, deep in our pelvis. In Western society physical strength is associated with upper body, arm and shoulder muscles rippling. In self-defence we spend our time bringing women's sense of their own energy downwards, learning to move and turn from the pelvis, visualising sources of power, learning that even as we explode our energy upwards in escaping a choke hold, as we strike forwards and upwards at an aggressor's chin, we are moving from a source of power low down in our bodies. Our voices can communicate this sense of power directly and devastatingly.

There is an element of surprise, time and again, as women report that they felt unable to do anything – but they screamed and he ran. The surprise can be partly physical shock, partly the surprise of interrupting his expectations. Our aggressor has a scenario in his mind, an image of compliant femininity. We can use our voices to reverse roles and take the initiative. When we fear we are being followed, rather than quickening our step and nervously looking over our shoulder we stop, turn, face the invader and ask what he wants. Our voices establish that after all we are able to take control and pull the rug out from under his feet.

Think about your own experiences: when have you used your voice to redirect a situation and get yourself out of trouble?

Women who are likely to be seen as particularly vulnerable targets find a special pleasure in tapping this source of power. Women with disabilities that affect their speech discover that what matters is not so much having their words understood as making sure that the message behind them is clear. The message is 'Don't mess with me!' The effect of speaking up for themselves can be dramatic. An elderly woman can doubly confuse an aggressor by giving an 'unladylike' roar.

Our voices project our energy outwards. They are part of beginning to think big, take up our place in the world. Like a bird protecting its territory with song, we can use our voices to mark out our space. We can insist that the supervisor at work who tries to slither around us keeps his distance; that the man next to us on the bus, trying to bulge into our seat, retreats to his own. Our voices are a crucial sign of the shift we may need to make from fear into anger. We can reassess incidents in which women 'couldn't do anything but scream' and see them not as examples of failure, of being unable to fight back, but as examples of women using one of our best weapons effectively. As we think about these screams, seeing them not just as cries for help but also as expressions of power, it becomes evident that they would be even more effective if we turned them from high pitched screams to strong, deep shouts of anger. Both fear and anger are vital responses to a sense of invasion. They trigger the same rush of adrenaline which can dramatically increase our thinking power and our fighting power.

Voices are not only for yelling. We explore our different spoken voices. Our voice can convey a sense of powerlessness: research has found that pleading is not effective in preventing rape. Pleading is very different from assertively saying what we do and don't want, making it clear from the tone of the voice that we are not only saying no, but meaning no. Sandra, from deep in her wheelchair, says 'No' in a tone that would stop a harasser dead in his tracks. For many of us this is by no means easy. It is often tone of voice that alerts a tutor to a woman's lack of self-esteem, to the amount of work she needs to do on building her belief that she has a right to set boundaries and find the resources within herself to do so.

We can use our voices as a way of deflecting violence, as an alternative to confrontation, an alternative to meeting aggression with aggression. All the time women are defusing situations, not by shouting back or cowering, but by firmly asserting their view of what is going on. A GP, asking advice from me about defence from violent patients, told me that in his experience it was male doctors, not female ones, who were more likely to be attacked. I suspect the difference here is that most women accumulate an unconscious knowledge of how not to escalate a situation while not giving in. Looking after children does teach us a thing or two. In self-defence sessions we are encouraging women to bring these skills to the surface and apply them to situations where they feel intimidated.

In a very different way, in talking about our experiences together we use our voices to break a major taboo – namely that women, like children, should be seen and not heard. We are led to believe that we should put up with intimidation and abuse in silence, turn away in embarrassment from remarks shouted at us, and believe threats as to what will happen to us if we let anyone else know about the private violence inflicted by someone who is supposed to love us. It is sometimes in self-defence classes that women first begin to speak of such abuse. They have found a safe environment where our shared fears are being brought out into the open, not to scare us more but to help us face the fear of violence and recognise that we can defend ourselves. They contrive to hide these terrible things not only from other people but often from themselves as well. Speaking about abuse is an early step on the road to healing. It is an act of rebellion all by itself. We may not be able to find our voices at the moment we need them, but that doesn't make us responsible for what has been happening. Speaking out afterwards is part of refusing to feel responsible, a forceful expression outwards, placing responsibility where it belongs – with the perpetrator.

This brings me to the wider context of our experience of self-defence, the deeper territory of the meaning of our voices. I believe that in using our voices powerfully we are challenging much that is taken for granted – taken for granted by ourselves, which makes change difficult for us, and taken for granted by others. So when we refuse to play by the accepted gender rules our resistance can be doubly effective.

In using our voices powerfully we are challenging notions of femininity that we have learnt as a route to acceptance in a society which systematically disempowers women. Our voices are an integral part of our physical selves. As with our bodies, we have learnt to use them in limited ways, observing limits set by society. Women's voices at their most 'feminine' are high, whispery, and appeasing, reflecting the conventional power relationship with men. Like our physical abilities, they can be expanded with daring and practice – once we feel prepared to challenge this socially dictated norm.

You can observe how the quality of the voice changes as part of women's socialisation. Early on in a self-defence course we will ask women to shout, all together. A group of young girls will raise the roof with an uninhibited roar: they love the excuse to let it out. But with groups of adult women we often have to dig down to find real voices underneath the squeaks and embarrassed titters they produce at first. As these women practise, using the strength of voice that they would normally use only when shouting at children, they are demonstrating to themselves and to the rest of the world that they are not always nice, polite, anxious to please and be liked. This can surprise them. It is the same unexpected challenge to an assumed power relationship that can astonish an attacker sufficiently for the woman to change the balance of power between them.

So much of this work is about challenging our socially created sense of powerlessness. If your experience as a child was of having your protests ignored by a powerful, abusing adult, you are not suddenly going to be able to shout 'No' as you practise your punches. 'No' is more than just a word. For a toddler, it is a satisfying assertion of her newly-discovered identity. But for a woman whose right to her own boundaries has been taken away, it can be one of the hardest things to say. We can only keep on encouraging her. Something inside begins to change as a woman's sense of her own worth and integrity grows. A quiet, determined 'No', or a huge roar belted out with a strike, can be the first sign of such a shift. You can pretend to punch or to kick. Women sometimes make the right arm movements, but with a pleasing smile on their faces and a total lack of conviction. But the pleasure accompanying the surge of power newly released through our voices is unmistakable and enormous.

The attitudes behind self-defence are a challenge to the social silencing of women. We are all familiar with the way men have taken up the airspace, from the tolerance given to noisy boys in the classroom through to the authoritative voices of male newsreaders and the well researched interruption of women by men, irrespective of the relationship between them. It has been observed that women doctors are interrupted by male patients more often than male doctors are. We are all familiar with the aggression and violence that women so often encounter from males. Yesterday on the bus a group of lads shouted 'Get yer tits out!' at a young woman who happened to be passing. An almost tangible silence rippled through the women in the bus. How amazing it is when a woman refuses to collude – when, for example, a young woman on a bus turns and announces to everyone on board that the man next to her is bothering her, that he is a dirty old pervert! He shrivels into his seat and gets off at the first opportunity.

Just as racist abuse can be a prelude to physical violence, so physical violence in relationships often follows on from verbal abuse. 'You're fat/lazy/loose/ugly/incompetent!' Male partners use their voices to establish and reinforce control, to undermine the woman and convince her she is worth nothing to anybody else. Women are silenced by their fear that answering back will only irritate and aggravate the problem, that it could precipitate a thumping.

Women who hope that silence will render them invisible and untouchable have found that a meek reaction can precipitate violence. For them the discovery of new ways to use their voices is especially powerful. Janet had left a violent husband years ago, but he could still terrorise her on his visits to pick up the children, marching into the house as though it was his own and turning it upside down when he felt like doing so. After experimenting with her voice in self-defence sessions she stopped him at the door, looked him straight in the eye and told him he was never coming in again, not without her permission. He began to bluster and she repeated herself in a low, calm voice, saying 'This is my home. Don't come any further.' He backed off and left seeming, as she reported afterwards, 'four foot seven instead of the six foot six he had always looked before.' Another woman in a similar situation first marked her refusal to be intimidated by telling her ex-husband clearly and firmly to take his shoes off before he came into the house. He did so and his power shrivelled in front of them both.

Our voices can also challenge assumptions about the *nature* of power. They can express a transformation in the way we relate to those around us. These women were not expressing the need to have power *over* someone, but simply to sense power *within themselves*. This concept is completely unfamiliar to people accustomed to getting their way by harassment, abuse and aggression. It is a challenge to the way society is organised – to the hierarchies in schools, families and workplaces, where lines of authority are maintained through 'power over' and the expected response of fear. A woman using her voice to assert herself is giving a very different response from the aggressive one that leads to fights, to a battle for 'power over' and a higher place in the pecking order. It is my impression that the police and judges are not aware of this distinction when they advise us 'Don't fight back, it only makes him angrier.' We can make the difference clear through the way we use our voices.

We can use our voices to challenge the feeling, in ourselves and others, that we are somehow to blame for the violence directed against us. We may know in our heads that we are not to blame, while not really feeling it. Finding our voices can be so powerful because they are a route not only outside into the world but inside, into our emotions. We often suppress rage at the way we have been treated, often in the belief that it might have been partly our fault, that we should have done more to stop it. Deidre, a severely disabled woman, had been assaulted by a carer. Punching into a bag, shouting 'No', she generated so much anger that it threatened to overwhelm her, but left her feeling that she had touched an emotion she had never allowed herself to feel before. This was part of coming to terms with what had happened, part of turning her emotion outwards, of placing the responsibility on her abuser, of healing the assault. As self-defence teachers we do not use voice as therapy: that is not our expertise. But we do recognise that using our voices to find and express our anger can be the first step to self-esteem, dropping the burden of guilt and setting out on the road to defending ourselves in the future.

'*Kee ai*', the shout used in martial arts, means 'release of the spirit' in Japanese. As our spirits become more confident, so we express through our voices. We hear ourselves and are astonished as we make our inner voice heard. We learn that as we change the way we use our voices, so we change ourselves. A growing sense of power flows back and forth on the waves of sound.

In coming back to my original questions, I think they share the same answer. The difficulty we experience in using our voices lies precisely in their challenge to the traditional distribution of power. In using our voices assertively we are not only summoning a crucial element of our physical effectiveness. We are having to overturn both our individual experience of powerlessness and all the ways in which women's voices collectively have been muted, silenced. As we break the taboos, let our voices rip, we share in the release of power experienced by those women who got together to voice their resistance in Northern Ireland, yelling as they banged dustbin lids to warn of army incursions into their communities; in Vittoria, Spain, where groups of women have taken action by marching into a bar, shouting the name of a rapist, shaming him off the streets; in apartheid South Africa, singing and yodelling defiantly at the funerals of people murdered by the state; and on women's Reclaim the Night marches, shouting 'Whatever we do, where ever we go, Yes means yes and No means no.' Not surprising that many of us find it difficult to use our voices powerfully and that it is so effective when we do!

The Voice of the Teacher

Roz Comins

Having worked for many years as a voice coach to actors
in training, it was a big shock to discover that teachers
often suffer from discomfort leading to quite serious
problems with their voices as a result of using them in the
school environment. Every year, numerous teachers need
treatment and therapy for loss of voice – problems which
actors would also suffer from if they didn't spend a lot of
time acquiring good voice habits at drama school.

Voice is a major part of an actor's training. Student
actors often believe their voices are adequate when they
enter drama school, but once they begin to work on them
they discover that the voice needs more attention. Then,
as their voices open up and strengthen, they begin to
acquire fresh qualities. When voice develops there is a
change in the person. You can hear and sense they are
getting closer to what the words are saying. This discovery
of the full range of the voice is in keeping with the whole
process of training an actor, enabling her/him to discover
natural skills in thinking, feeling, moving and speaking,
focusing them in order to create a character that will
convince and move an audience in the theatre.

Starting in 1988, I was involved in a project with the
Voice Research Society (now the British Voice Association)
looking into the whole subject of vocal disabilities in the
teaching profession: how these came about and what could
be done to improve the situation. Our researches were
carried out informally in the setting of practical
workshops which were offered to any teachers who

wanted to know about voice care. We discovered that a large number of teachers suffered from serious loss of voice. The majority of them were women. We found teachers at primary level who could no longer sing: either the pitch of their voices had a very limited range or they suffered from sore throats. A few who took part in an early workshop had voices that were so hoarse and harsh that I could not believe they were expected to carry on without having anything done about it. By the end of the school week some of the teachers could hardly speak at all.

'But, Roz,' said other voice teachers who came along to help, 'their voices are dreadful!' This was not spoken in criticism but concern. My speech and language therapist colleagues had already recognised that many of the teachers had no idea how their voice was produced. Once they understood the mechanism that actors learn about in their training, a lot of them were able to get a handle on their problems and their voices were transformed. But there were others whose problems were so serious that they needed medical help. Some were seriously thinking of cutting their careers short and leaving the profession if they could not find a solution.

The impact of these discoveries resulted in speech and language therapists and voice teachers meeting and working together for the first time. We were not drama teachers or singers, but people concerned with working the speaking voice. I recall the excitement of seven voice teachers sitting round a table talking together. Through the study of individual voice patients and a series of investigative workshops we began to develop the Voice Care Network. Our aim was to enable people to recognise that voice is at the heart of the teaching and learning process, that it is essential to communication in all spoken languages and that the quality of a voice can have a powerful effect on those who listen to it. Speech work with only limited emphasis on voice had slipped out of teacher training in the 1970s. We knew of only four institutions where it was still on the curriculum. But every step we took led closer to the obvious conclusion that work on voice must be established as an essential part of Initial Teacher Training (ITT).

We began with a study. Speech and language therapists in the Midlands found that over 30 per cent of patients in some voice clinics were teachers. We decided to begin by offering exploratory voice workshops to practising teachers. Some Teachers' Centres agreed to provide space for workshops and distribute publicity to local schools. The response from teachers was enthusiastic. Schools requested workshops even though voice was not a recognised topic for in-service training. A learning process had begun.

There are about 450,000 teachers in the UK, with the number of women exceeding men by roughly two to one. Each year around 20,000 new entrants come into teaching from Postgraduate Certificate of Education (PGCE) courses and a further 12,000 from first degree courses. The institutions and schools in which they train are spread all over the UK and Open University PGCEs are scattered even more widely. Our task was enormous. The project required much more than a team of voice practitioners to run workshops: a sustained initiative by a group of professionals with clear objectives was needed to gather the evidence and demonstrate what could be done. We needed to study teachers' voice problems and find out precisely how these related to oral skills and classroom management. We were also convinced that effective voices were of vital importance to the children who had to listen and learn from them.

By circulating information, responding to enquiries about workshops and sending booklets to those we couldn't reach we laid the foundations of the Voice Care Network. We also set up interactive study meetings to encourage more experienced voice teachers and speech and language therapists to join us, as we didn't want to be asked for workshops and be unable to meet requests. Through these meetings we added to our knowledge and moved towards a sense of unity which was helped by the circulation of our newsletter *Voice Matters*. Today the network is a registered charity with over 200 members, of which 100 are tutors, located all over Britain.

Inevitably there is a political aspect to the Voice Care Network. At one point the Health and Safety Executive, impressed by our case, put voice care on an agenda but took no action. We approached an under secretary of state. He told us that he was aware that effective voice production was one of a range of communication skills teachers were expected to have, but such decisions were a matter for the training institutions. In reply we pointed out the high cost of teachers' voice problems. A supply teacher replacing one who has to take a day off sick is paid about £100 a day. Add to this the cost of medical care, the personal loss to a teacher who cannot teach and the waste of training for those who leave the profession altogether, and a short, professionally prepared voice session is cheap in comparison.

However, they were to need much more persuasion. In 1996 a government circular stated that teachers' competencies needed to include the ability to establish clear expectations of behaviour and appropriate discipline from their students. In response to this the Voice Care Network (together with the English Speaking Board and the Society of Drama Teachers) pointed out to the Teacher Training Agency that none of these aims could be achieved with poorly managed and ineffective vocal technique: teachers should have access to effective training in voice and oral skills. At the same time we made contact with directors of Schools of Education. We explained that voice work does not imply phonetic precision or the imposition of upper class accents like Eliza in Shaw's *Pygmalion*. Neither is it simply a process for treating inadequate voices. The voice is the channel for communication in words: it is as important to the spoken word as the pen is for writing. A voice that has flexibility and stamina can heighten a teacher's professional skill, whatever the accent or language, because skilful interactive talk is at the core of teaching. However, we were met with statements about shortage of time and shortage of funds at almost every turn.

The teachers' unions, on the other hand, responded enthusiastically. One union handed us 50 letters they had received from members with voice problems. One letter told of a teacher who had acquired a bull's larynx from a butcher in order to study the cause of her problem. Another union made an appeal to a Department of Social Security tribunal on behalf of a nursery teacher who had given up work when she lost her voice. The appeal failed: loss of voice was not a registered industrial injury! A third union, the Professional Association of Teachers (PAT), prepared statements and evidence for a dedicated primary school teacher whose voice had been reduced to a whisper so that she had had to leave the profession she loved. In September 1994 the DSS tribunal decided that she had lost her voice through work and that she had therefore suffered 'an accident at work' within the meaning of the DSS regulations. On top of her regular work, this teacher had been responsible for the school's Christmas concerts on two successive years. The tribunal accepted that the two concerts were examples of specific incidents by which the voice had been damaged. If this woman had known about voice care all this might have been prevented. The solicitor for PAT made sure that all reports of the tribunal in the press, on television and radio emphasised the need for teachers to have voice training to support their work in schools. In fact, PAT has consistently supported the case for voice training within ITT.

*

When planning our workshops we knew that while actors and teachers have to cope with stress, their environments and the demands on their voices are very different. The actor has a text, the teacher improvises. The actor's body is trained, while often the teacher hardly knows how to relax. The audience pays to enjoy a performance, the pupils are obliged to attend. The audience claps, but pupils rarely applaud. The actor can use emotion freely in playing a part, the teacher must keep a firm grip on emotion. The actor has costume and set, the teacher has a blackboard and visual aids. The actor is supported by front of house staff, playwright, director and specialist back stage staff. The teacher is also the script writer, director, set designer, usherette, scene shifter, catering manager, publicity manager, box office and bouncer. Student teachers can add to this list the roles of policewoman, social worker, comedienne, clown, disciplinarian, Ms Angry and Everyone's Best Friend.

However, voice training as it has been devised for actors over decades can be adapted to support the teacher's role in school. The figure on p129 summarises the main areas of work, showing how the interrelated elements come together. It is rooted firmly in practical voice work used in theatre schools and is known as the Wave Diagram.

The diagram takes its name from sound waves radiating from their source. The work it represents begins with the person in the centre and develops through the inner waves to the periphery, from control of the voice to effective oral communication, from the medium to the message. Skills developed in one wave support the others. Learning can equally well begin on the outside with existing skills. The speaker's intentions must always be involved. As voice is bound up in the person, work on voice and on the self overlap.

VCN workshops are held in schools and universities in every kind of space you can imagine. As few as 8 students or up to 200 may attend. Sessions may run for an hour or for

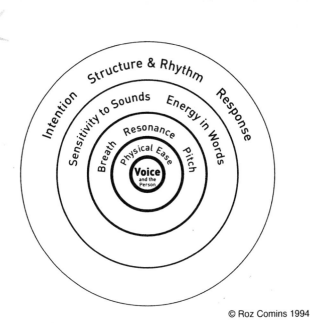

© Roz Comins 1994

a whole day. Sometimes in the course of a year 1000 students will be divided into groups of 40 to attend a two-hour practical voice workshop. Follow-ups are rare, in contrast to actors who have regular voice classes and tutorials throughout their training.

We plan the session to encourage teachers to be more aware of voice and how it is produced. We want them to be aware of what happens when words are spoken, how the voice flows through the changing shapes and movements of the mouth while the mind perceives their meaning, and how there is often a relationship between the thought and the sounds that are made. Teachers need to know that when voice is produced efficiently it keeps in good condition. Vocal health advice includes two essentials: the need to drink water in order to lubricate the larynx and the need to take care when suffering from laryngitis. Laryngitis is a great test: the proper treatment is rest and recuperation, but since this is seldom an option, teaching methods have to be rigorously adapted until the voice has completely recovered.

Workshops need to be refreshing and create a sense of exploration. How does voice work? How do we control it? What else can it do? The workshop is a master class in which to discover more about the voice and its potential. Often people do not realise that the muscles of the larynx are very intricate. Their primary job is to protect the airway. We use them to cough when anything goes the 'wrong way', and we close the vocal folds (or cords) to hold our breath or to summon up maximum strength when we lift or push heavy weights and objects. When we release emotion by laughing and crying, the larynx is in good shape and the muscles are balanced, but when we are distressed and tense there may be some constriction which can produce the sensation of a lump in the throat. Because muscles of the larynx are affected by tension and stress, the pitch of our voices often goes up when we are nervous.

In the workshops we relate voice theory to practice. In the dual roles of speech therapist and voice teacher we perform a double-act, going from explanation to practical work in order to negotiate the areas shown in the wave diagram. We expect our students to experience releasing the breath and then allowing it to be taken in again of its own volition. Exercises for easy alignment of posture and to free the vocal tract help teachers to identify small mannerisms. Voice efficiency is reduced by holding the voice in the throat, or keeping it back with a tense jaw, lifting the chin, or constantly twisting the neck towards the class while working at the blackboard. Each of these affects voice quality.

We consider pitch. Every voice has a natural range of pitch. Women's voices are closer to the pitch of their pupils' voices than men's and in seeking a contrast they instinctively pitch up their voices. When men open their mouths the pitch may be six to eight notes lower than the prevailing notes of a primary school so it is easier for them to be heard.

Tone of voice conveys feeling or emotion. A single workshop allows limited time to think about words. Barbara Woodhouse's dog training 'Si—T!' is a short cut to demonstrate how words can work. But how do our brains categorise words? We may quote Chomsky or Steven Pinker, who believe that our brains are wired for grammar. Speculating about the early development of language we may mention Mike Beaken, who has a theory that it evolved in the process of discussing tool making, or Robin Dunbar, who suggested that our first ancestors may have engaged in mutual grooming like apes and as our brains developed this was replaced by verbal grooming.

A workshop always includes a voice warm-up that the teachers can use daily before entering their classrooms. We ensure that anyone who needs personal advice is encouraged to speak individually with the speech and language therapist. Workshop participants are asked to fill in a questionnaire before the workshop gets going as it is helpful to have their voice needs described clearly and openly. During the workshop, participants want to talk about their pupils' listening, the reading of stories, acoustics, background noise and difficulties over discipline. In looking for solutions we become catalysts. Teachers analyse the problems and we share our ideas. Lively comments are voiced about noise and about open plan classrooms where it can be difficult to focus on activities.

Back in the classroom after attending our workshops, teachers have reported putting some of these thoughts into action. Having expressed regret that shouting was the only way some pupils conversed, one teacher got her pupils to explore quiet voices, friendly voices and the playground voice. A reception class did an imaginative exercise in which they were asked to explore the noise a sound made when it escaped from their teacher's pocket. Classes explored movements in relation to active verbs. Primary teachers began to involve their pupils in voice warm-ups. Thus language learning was beginning with the spoken word as opposed to the written word, as David Crystal has suggested it should. Primary singing was another hurdle. Teachers were being affected badly by singing loudly at uncomfortable pitches. Later a teacher told me, 'I encouraged them to sing alone this week. They were very quiet, but they sounded beautiful!'

At one workshop I asked a small group to record a sample of their teaching voices. I played back the tape and out came one strong stereotypical 'teacher voice'! Teaching all day encourages this. The voice becomes hard, too high or too low, even robotic. Often this is accompanied by a stiff jaw and stiff shoulders. One teacher admitted that she ground her teeth in her sleep because of worries that she might not complete the curriculum in time. Another caring teacher was struggling with unmanageable boys in a lively class. She had just 13 days left before the end of term brought relief. By the end of the workshop the muscles standing out on her neck released and her voice became easy. I was deeply impressed with the way teachers applied the work, released their stiffness, improved their breathing, paused more, slowed down and reduced unnecessary talk. Some even managed to regain notes in their singing voices.

Secondary teachers had problems specific to the subjects they taught. Teachers of PE and swimming often lost their voices and needed help. We discussed voice and the possible use of other means of communication which can be as simple as a drum, a castanet, a tone bar or some kind of rattle to stop the action before speaking. Teachers of Modern Languages who had to talk for a lot of the time were encouraged to work on easy posture, pausing and remembering to breathe. Science teachers were coached for clear speech and ability to get immediate attention. Art

Technology teachers learnt to release more resonance. Teachers of Information and Communication Technology worked on how to be heard in a room full of computers and were reminded to drink plenty of water when rooms were overheated. Confidence was built for teachers who needed to take whole-school assemblies and for younger staff who were nervous about talking to parents. 'At last,' one teacher wrote, 'we are finally speaking to people who recognise that there can be problems!' Teaching is stressful. The exercises were designed to strengthen and improve voice quality, but they also have the side effect of reducing stress.

In general, student voices are flexible and very few have serious voice problems before they begin teaching. With them, voice awareness sessions are run on similar lines to those described above with emphasis on voice care and practical voice production. Usually an institution invites us to do just one workshop. But at one university where I work, over 20 students every year attend a six-week voice skills course. Rapport is established and Friday afternoons become a refreshing reinforcement of the introductory session. Students lie on the floor to relax and breathe. Then humming begins and turns to a magnificent mixture of choral tones. The sound quality changes as consonants are babbled fast and slow, with rising and falling voices. During the course individual students make specific requests for help. Some for whom English is not their mother tongue need to improve their pronunciation. Other students want to strengthen a weak voice, to monitor a loud voice or to avoid monotony. An 's' sound may need strengthening or an 'r' may need to be worked on. Faulty pronunciation is something that pupils pick on and mimic, creating a diversion that upsets the smooth running of a class.

In preparation for work in school they let their voices flow through lines from Martin Luther King's 'I have a dream'. They check each other's breathing and how the words carry. To exercise their ability to command, the Prince's speech from *Romeo and Juliet* is used. When they touch the hand of the next student while speaking a line from a poem, they notice how voice quality changes. They practise entering the classroom to get attention, praising the class, reprimanding the class and setting homework concisely. A camcorder is set to work and the recording is played back for discussion. Warm-ups are created and remembered for use before teaching.

At the end of the PGCE courses, feedback on school placements can be difficult to get as the students become involved in interviews, accept teaching posts and leave the area. From what we have heard students do recognise the benefits of voice skills sessions. Students with challenging classes now notice when 'crowd control' takes over from voice control in moments of crisis and learn how to cope. Discipline problems can be inherited from previous teachers. One student asked for troublesome pupils to be temporarily removed. On top of this she learnt some techniques from a senior police officer which helped her to deal with the situation. She had gained from attending the voice skills course, but the hurdles she faced in the classroom were much tougher. Perhaps research may find learning methods more suited to restless pupils who are struggling to mature. But many PGCE students came through school placements with satisfaction. A young teacher of Modern Languages was congratulated on her dramatic reading aloud, and one teaching Information Technology said, 'There were no problems for me. If there was a noise I just clapped my hands and asked them to be quiet'.

As the tutors in the VCN continue to work together we increasingly grow to trust in the effectiveness of the work we are doing. We are convinced that the workshops create greater awareness and more insight. We are aware that the work can lower stress levels and increase the confidence and self-esteem of those who attend and feedback confirms this.

The experience of taking part in them encourages teachers to recognise more fully that voice conveys far more than facts on paper. When we allow our voices to ring with joy we can create joy in those who listen to us. The experience of singing in a group or listening to a choir can, as most of us have found, be deeply moving. George Eliot wrote that voice goes deeper into us than other things. Thomas Hardy wrote of his wife after her death, 'Woman much missed, how you call to me, call to me . . . ' The sound of a voice can remind us of all that we feel or know about a person. Without the voice, words have no sound. Just as our bodies work better when they are kept supple and active, the same applies to our minds and our voices. If we use the voice as a tool, it needs to be kept in good condition. If we wield it as a weapon, it is two-edged. If we use it as an instrument to promote learning, ideas can be brought to life and imagination has no bounds.

When Communities Find a Voice

Jenny Goodman

I have been working with voice and song in community settings for almost a decade, but the seeds of this involvement were probably sown much earlier in my life – not even in my twenties, but way back in childhood. It didn't come primarily from my parents, who loved classical music, nor from my sister, whose addiction to the Walker Brothers gave me another perspective. It was the direct result of geographical influence, of having spent my early years in a village in the Colne Valley in West Yorkshire, a stone's throw from Huddersfield.

To say that choral singing and music were important in that community is an understatement. Every Sunday I sat in the Congregational Church, facing the choir that was ranked above the pulpit, as those substantial Yorkshire women and men belted the hymns at us. Every Whitsun we walked through the village behind the brass bands. My best friend's dad was a leading light in one of these brass bands. Every year, the school where my father taught (and where my sisters studied) produced a cracking version of some Gilbert and Sullivan operetta. And at my own primary school I learnt songs from various traditions, ranging from Scottish folk to calypso, courtesy of my music teacher and schools' radio.

This was a living musical tradition closely linked to the working class, socialist traditions of the area. What I remember about the church choir was the lusty singing, not the elitism that many people associate with church going. This impression was, no doubt, reinforced by my family's values, as my mother was brought up with the values of the Methodist Church and my dad was a die-hard socialist who came to Yorkshire to teach in one of the very first comprehensive schools because he believed in equal opportunity for everyone.

Nevertheless I have only recently realised that I have come full circle. Apart from that Yorkshire village, my experience of music for a long time was within the classical tradition. Once we moved to Northumberland I continued to sing in choirs and operettas at school, learnt the clarinet and sang in the church choir, but I began to encounter the phrase 'Yes, well, she likes music, but she's not really talented'. I wasn't musical *enough*, whatever that means! Music became a source of pressure – something that involved exams and competition and understanding what a diminished fourth was and how to count 6/8 time. I always sang but as it had 'rejected' me first, I resisted becoming part of the musically talented elite. I am glad of this now – it means that my voice was never properly trained in the classical tradition, so I haven't had the struggle some friends have had in finding their natural voices after a classical training.

I carried on singing in choirs through university and after I moved to London, but then things began to change. First I decided to be a solo artist (a star!) and went for singing lessons with a woman who specialised in jazz. She encouraged me to experience as much singing as I could and voice workshops soon became my favourite haunt. I listened to Sweet Honey in the Rock (see Chapter 4) and realised that beautiful and amazing singing could also be about expressing your values and political beliefs. Consequently I joined a political street choir called Raised Voices. Singing had suddenly become something totally different – or was I just returning to my roots? Singing was about fun, it was about creativity, it could express your political beliefs. There were songs from South Africa that blew my mind. There were harmonies so rich I wanted to die of joy. Although we worked from sheet music in Raised Voices, there was a wonderful sense that those who were more expert than you were there to pass on their skills, not to put you down for not understanding what they meant about a song being in the key of D.

Meanwhile I was now employed as a community worker, a job that matched my values of empowering people and challenging the inequalities of the status quo. I worked initially in housing and then moved into more generic, neighbourhood based community development work. I was discovering the power of campaigning to build people's confidence and skills and, conversely, the fact that confidence, skills and power can be gained by working in a group. I became more and more interested in groups. At the same time I was becoming less interested in community development as such, mainly because I was exhausted by it. My experience of singing was making me realise that I got energy from being creative with others, while the open-ended nature of the community develop-ment work drained me. I enjoyed the sense of satisfaction that came from having a finished product – ie a song.

I decided to do a community work course to give myself time out to reflect on my practice and look at the possibilities of a change of direction. I wanted to move towards adult education, to do some work with women and with creativity. Since community work courses in England tended to focus heavily on youth and community work, I moved to Scotland where there were courses combining adult education, youth work and community development. I specialised in adult education and community arts and my final placement was in a community arts project on a housing scheme on the outskirts of Edinburgh.

Here in Wester Hailes I used the arts as an educational tool in a community setting for the first time. The approach was firmly rooted in the best community education practice – focusing on giving people an opportunity to develop their skills and confidence within a group setting – but within a creative context. Those who took part were encouraged to explore their own experiences and validate them through creative expression. Great care and attention were given to the process: being aware of group dynamics and roles and working with themes chosen by group members. There was also the additional ingredient of working towards a finished product. Performances and exhibitions were an essential part of the process, with an emphasis on excellence: community arts was not to be seen as 'second best'.

People in Wester Hailes were accustomed to being regarded as worthless, with no skills and no talent. Any worthwhile work in this community had to challenge that experience. There was also a desire to educate the wider world to the reality of living on the estate, challenging the stereotypical views perpetrated by the media in Edinburgh and beyond.

Drama was the main focus of the project. Initially I joined them as a development worker with a young people's drama group, but I was itching to try developing some work around singing and my first experiment was to set up a community choir. We began with a set of voice and song taster workshops in which I took my first shaky steps as a voice workshop leader, combining my knowledge about devising sessions with vocal techniques I had learnt from Frankie Armstrong. The workshops developed into a regular weekly group with mixed success. People were keen, but the group was small and this left unconfident singers feeling exposed and unsupported: it meant that our repertoire was limited because not all members of the group were confident enough to hold parts alone or even in pairs. My intention was to negotiate with the group over the choice of material to work with, but the range of taste was huge and not necessarily compatible. Since I had no skills as an arranger we sang mostly in unison when people were thirsting for harmonies. However, the group survived and managed to develop. We were eventually drawn into a project to devise a soundtrack for a tape and slide presentation around the theme 'A Day in the Life of Wester Hailes'. Workshops on songwriting led to the creation of original material which was recorded with much hilarity in the recording studios at the local school. The night of the premier was a very special event, leaving everyone with a huge sense of accomplishment.

By this time I had a deep rooted belief that the free use of the voice and singing was integral to human well-being. I had witnessed the sheer pleasure people got from singing together, the way it could bond people as a group and the release people experienced when they discovered, after years of criticism, that they *could* sing. That this experience promoted health and confidence was self-evident. People with asthma found their breathing was easier. Others talked about their increased confidence to speak out in other situations because they felt easier with the power and effectiveness of their voices. This seemed to be particularly true of the women in the group, whose confidence blossomed visibly through the free and strong use of their voices in song.

The Wester Hailes experience led me to think carefully about the elements which must be present in a workshop to make singing and voice work safe and joyful. I realised that I needed a repertoire of songs with which I felt comfortable, ranging from very simple to more complex. I found the inspiration I needed at a Women's Singing Week at Laurieston Hall where I learnt songs from a variety of traditions including African, East European and Native American. I began to understand the freedom that can be found when singing in a language which is not your own, how this can sink you in the sensuality of words and sound in a way that is not so easy in your own tongue. I was also made aware again of the huge diversity of ways in which the voice is used throughout the world and of the fact that a woman's singing voice is not limited to stereotypical sweet and light 'feminine' sounds, but can be powerful, harsh, deep and strong. It was during the week at Laurieston that I began to explore for myself a far deeper singing voice than I had used before, revelling in the rich vibrations it released.

One woman taught us spirituals and gospel songs she had learnt in a workshop with Ysaye Barnwell of Sweet Honey in the Rock. I rushed off and bought Ysaye's teaching tapes. The historical background she included on the tapes gave me a deeper understanding and respect for the songs and clarified my ideas of how singing could work as a tool for building a community. When song is an organic part of community life there is no room for the idea that some people are non-singers: it is simply assumed that everyone takes part. Singing in harmony can be taken as symbolic of the way healthy communities work: its beauty is created not by uniformity but by diversity. And it works only if there is sensitive listening and respect for each part and for its contribution to the whole.

When I returned from Laurieston I had the opportunity to devise a programme around voice and song for Theatre Workshop in Edinburgh. I decided to run a series of weekly workshops over a period of six weeks, starting with two sessions of 'freeing the voice' and developing confidence, followed by four sessions learning songs from different parts of the world. The workshops were a huge success and were repeated a number of times. The experiment worked well: people were not committing themselves to an on-going group and they didn't seem to want negotiation: they just wanted to come and sing together! As ever I gave careful attention to building trust in the group so that people could sing freely. In these workshops I began to notice some interesting gender differences. Men were more likely to be tight in their bodies, the tightness limiting their vocal freedom and resonance: a loss of confidence in their voices seemed to go back to puberty when the voice breaks. Women were far less confident about making 'big' sounds: again and again I saw the liberation women experienced in discovering their calling voice. I remember one woman, who had previously experienced herself as being 'unable to sing', standing by the open window while we vocalised together: her eyes were tightly shut and she was calling and calling with a look of total ecstasy on her face.

All these influences and thoughts came together when I was approached by Edinburgh District Council to create a community choir for the European Summit in 1992 which would sing songs from around the world. By now I knew exactly what I wanted to do and how. I wanted to create a community of song where everyone was welcome, regardless of their previous experience or confidence. This would be a choir that worked to the principle that everyone can sing. Certain key elements had to be in place for this to work. First, I needed good numbers so that less confident singers would find their voices supported and not feel exposed. This was resolved when around 100 people turned up for the first night. Second, people would be encouraged to sing whichever parts they chose. This meant we had women singing low and men singing high. Third, everything would be taught by ear to rid people of the concept that they can only sing if they can read a piece of paper. This condition returns people to the original and most basic way that human beings learn both to talk and to sing – by imitation and repetition. Fourth, I wanted to take people away from the concept that only a certain type of smooth, sweet sound was acceptable or even natural and help them to appreciate that the human voice has many textures and qualities. This was achieved by teaching songs from a variety of cultures where diverse vocal qualities were used. In this way Voice House was born and continues to this day, still with around 100 members.

By this point my working life had fallen into a pattern of working part time as a freelance voice and song specialist and being employed part time in women's community projects. My voice and song work was never focused solely on women, but it was often women's groups that asked me to do workshops. I am always conscious in working with any group that there is an opportunity to build self-esteem as well as have a good sing. When I work with women an important element, again, is the chance to make a lot of noise – a favourite exercise is throwing tantrums, as if the need to stamp and yell has been repressed. When I choose women's songs to work with I draw particularly on traditions where the voice is used powerfully and on songs which combine strong vocal use with physical movement. Call and response songs are always popular and groups will go over these again and again. I tend not to do exercises which involve improvisation with groups that are not confident unless I work with them over a longer period – either a whole day or over a number of weeks – because it induces self-consciousness. Simple songs and chants, however, work quickly and give instant satisfaction.

Recently I have stopped freelancing and begun to work full time as the co-ordinator of a project directed towards women who face the greatest barriers to returning to the labour market: women who have been unemployed for a long time, single parents, women with no formal qualifications, black women and women with disabilities. We aim to build their confidence and I have been able to use my voice work with groups as part of that process. Meanwhile I am also concentrating on Voice House and my own performances. The power of working to free the voice as a tool for building self-esteem continues to amaze and delight me. Recently I sang at a Christmas party for the women's project – the song to which everyone sang along with great gusto was 'Wild Women Don't Get the Blues!' This wild woman has happily returned to the lusty singing of her Yorkshire childhood.

The Sound of Stories

Jenny Pearson

Twenty years ago it seemed as if the voice of the traditional storyteller was vanishing from the land. Otherwise, stories were kept on bookshelves, read silently with the eyes and occasionally aloud, mostly to children – until the children were able to read quietly to themselves. They were read over the radio and dramatised for performance on television. But apart from occasional stories told at folk clubs and festivals, by idiosyncratic characters like Ken Campbell, the authentic sound of the storyteller's voice, re-weaving the magic of a tale in the moment, was becoming a wonder of the past.

Then something happened. Deep in the collected psyche, a need reawakened and a lot of people began to ask 'Where are the storytellers?' A television series called *The Storyteller*, featuring John Hurt as a teller of traditional tales, drew a wide audience: though an actor performing a story script is not the real thing, John Hurt's storyteller was spell binding. Meanwhile, at a grassroots level, those of us in whom the need was particularly strong had already begun to take matters into our own hands. Some of us told stories among ourselves, experimenting to see if we could reinvent the storyteller's art. A group called the College of Storytellers was beginning to attract an audience to regular evenings of storytelling in a London pub. A multi-cultural group of storytellers and musicians had got going under the name of Common Lore, performing mainly in schools. A man called Roberto Lagnado, inspired by some storytellers he had encountered on holiday in Morocco, told some stories in London schools and was so popular with the children that the Inner London Education Authority employed him as a peripatetic storyteller on a teacher's salary. Then a young man called Ben Haggarty beat a drum in the Portobello market and declared to the astonished crowd, 'After many years, a storyteller has come to tell you some stories!' Ben went on to create the West London Storytelling Unit with Daisy Keble and Tuup, a London born, Guyanese drummer and storyteller, and they toured Britain with programmes for adult audiences as well as children. These were the first heady years of a 'storytelling revival' which is now all over Britain, with countless storytelling clubs and a handful of festivals every year.

So what is the particular magic of a story that is told? What was it that we were all missing so badly that we turned our backs on the more representational storytelling of the twentieth century to rediscover the ancient art of spinning narrative gold out of the straw of imagination? Every storyteller probably has a different answer to these questions. However, it is my guess that most answers would point to the theme of imagination and the part it can play in refreshing our sense of connection with the world. The traditional stories we tell transport us into a different landscape from the one we inhabit in our daily lives – a landscape that lies close to the 'savage and beautiful' country of dreams, as the Jungian analyst Alan McGlashen pointed out in his book *The Savage and Beautiful Country*. The forests and rivers, the kings and princesses and monsters and talking animals we encounter there, have a numinous quality, very like the places and creatures in a dream landscape. A traditional story can reflect our fears and conflicts at a very deep level, as well as our wishes: coming to the end of a story that has touched us in the depths can bring about an extraordinary feeling of arrival and peace, a feeling that something important has been resolved. These ancient stories have been passed carefully down the generations because people valued them as a source of comfort and wisdom, as well as entertainment. Those that have survived through time have done so because they have been 'top of the pops' for centuries. So why wouldn't we need them today?

For many of us, rediscovering the power and magic of told stories has been a homecoming. I knew from the beginning that something important was happening to me as I began to involve myself in the process of finding, learning and telling a traditional story. Previously, I had worked for some years as a journalist, first on a national newspaper then freelance. Typing my 'stories' in a silent room at home and dropping them into a postbox, I had come to feel that my words were vanishing into a void. TH White once said that a writer was someone sitting in a darkened room calling out 'Can anybody hear me?' That was just how it felt. Then a friend invited me to a storytelling evening where a woman told the story of *The Frog Prince*. I experienced transformation. Somehow, she became the frog looking up at me from the well and I was the princess, desperate to recover my golden ball. I lived the story. My first thought was 'I could listen to this for ever'. Afterwards I emerged from my trance and thought 'I must *do* this!'

So began my enthralment to the sound of stories. Looking through Grimms Fairy Tales for a story I could work on myself, I came to a stop at *Rapunzel*. I knew this was the one, though I didn't know why. I just kept going back to it, reading with great concentration, until the images had branded themselves on my mind – and then I realised that I knew it well enough to try telling it. It wasn't until I actually told *Rapunzel*, finding the words within me and sounding them with my voice, that my connection to the story was established and I found myself living it fully. I remember speaking those words near the end: 'Two of her tears fell on his eyes and suddenly they were clear and he could see again.' The image went straight to my heart. Thinking about it afterwards, I remembered EM Forster's 'Only connect'. People who heard it were moved, too. It was my first experience in storytelling of the way tears are not necessarily about being sad: they can mean we are in touch with what Hopkins termed 'the dearest freshness deep down things'. I recognised that here was a shared meaning, a meeting point beyond the merely personal. We were simultaneously touching base with one another and with something beyond ourselves. It felt like coming alive or waking up after a long sleep.

My discovery of storytelling had two immediate results. I was determined to get more of it and I was convinced that what stories were doing for me they could also do for others. I hired a room in a small community arts centre and started the Kew Storytellers. A nucleus of people came from the original storytelling evenings (which had come to an end as an 'adult education' course) plus a few locals whose curiosity was aroused by our publicity. We met once a week and gradually the numbers grew. In 1984 Frank Delaney featured us in a BBC radio series called *Telling Tales* and the broadcast brought along some more people who felt drawn towards traditional storytelling.

In those days we were asking among ourselves 'What is the art of storytelling? What exactly are we trying to do? How should it sound?' The group was experimental. We didn't go in for rules, except one. Very early on, we decided to ban books from the room. This was a vital step. The less confident among us had been clinging to books and *reading*, not telling, their stories. Some of us had come far enough along the road to recognise that reading aloud *sounds* different from telling a story in your own words. The effect of the ban on books was exciting. Stories came alive. A young Swedish woman called Anna, who had been struggling in her halting English to read and learn a rather sophisticated story by Saki, told us a simple tale she had been told by her grandmother and how, on certain nights, her grandmother would put a saucer of milk out on the doorstep 'for the fairies'. The impact was immediate: Anna had us eating out of her hand.

The ban on books rescued several people who had been feeling inadequate to the task in hand. When you have to reach inside yourself for a story, you find something more than the story – you begin to find your own voice as a storyteller. Over many years of running story groups and workshops, I have watched so many people making this discovery and it always thrills me. The moment of self-discovery is so often the moment when a storyteller finds the key to deep communication with those who are listening. This is the connection without which no amount of dramatic skill or verbal pyrotechnics can help you to touch the hearts of your audience.

We were becoming aware of big differences between the storyteller's art and the writer's. Book stories are more wordy than told stories. They can go in for adjectives and descriptions on a scale that would destroy the impact of a story that is told. This is partly because telling a story takes much longer, word for word, than reading with the eyes: a long description can easily 'lose' your audience. Descriptions and digressions can also break up the underlying pattern and rhythm that holds the connection between teller and listeners. Besides, the storyteller is less dependent on verbal description because she/he has the incomparable instrument of the voice with which to convey atmosphere, colour and mood. A seasoned storyteller learns to balance sound and structure in a way that holds the audience and at the same time gives the teller full scope to delight and surprise them. The sound of a story well told can reverberate around the back rooms of memory like music, sometimes for years. In some respects, storytelling is closer to music than to literature.

Our experimental phase at Kew taught us a lot about the art form we were trying to reinvent in the early eighties. In the beginning we told stories from many sources, including literature and even the newspapers. The experiments were fun, but over time it became strikingly clear that the old, magical tales of the oral tradition were the ones that worked best – the folk fairy tales and legends collected by researchers like the brothers Grimm in Germany, Perrault in France, and Joseph Jacobs in our own islands. These were the stories we found most satisfying, both as tellers and as listeners. We were reversing the process of the old collectors, lifting off the page the stories they had set down in print, bringing them back to life in our own words.

A useful guide for this process was a book published back in 1942 by the American storyteller Ruth Sawyer, called *The Way of the Storyteller*. She advises that 'stories must be acquired by long contemplation, by bringing the imagination to work, constantly, intelligently upon them. And finally by that power to blow life into them. And the method? That of learning incident by incident, picture by picture. Never word by word.'

While it was valuable to have a brief, anarchic time exploring the roots of storytelling for ourselves, it was wonderful when we caught up with the fact that the storyteller's art was still vigorously alive in remoter parts of our own islands, most particularly among the travelling people of Ireland and Scotland. I remember meeting Duncan Williamson, the great storyteller from the Scottish traveller tradition, in Battersea at Ben Haggarty's first International Festival of Storytelling in 1985. Duncan said with some indignation, 'What's this about a story-telling revival? How can you revive something that has never died?'

Duncan has also said, 'Storytelling is like painting with words. The pictures in my mind are transferred into your

mind. The most important thing in telling a story is to keep the picture clear. If you lose it, your audience loses it, too. '
Listening to Duncan's stories, it becomes quite clear how this 'visual transmission' of story scenes can come about with very little verbal description. When he speaks of a castle, a mountain, a wave on the shore, I am able to see it with the inward eye of imagination through the conviction in his voice. The mountain may not be the same in every detail as the one he is seeing, because it is shaped by my memories and experience of mountains. But his voice communicates it as something *present* and this is all I need to be able to see the mountain for myself.

It was the travelling people of Scotland who finally showed me the authentic sound of stories as they have been told at the fireside down the centuries. We owe it to their separateness from society, to their poverty and their unquenchable appetite for freedom, that they have kept their heritage of stories and songs alive until now. Travelling the country with their families in search of farm work through the summers and holing up in communal encampments through the winter, their only entertainment of an evening was stories and songs around a communal fire and music played on the instruments they carried along with them. Duncan has described their life in the introduction to his first book, *Fireside Tales of the Traveller Children*, and so has Betsy Whyte in her autobiography, *The Yellow on the Broom*. Possibly the first story to hit the charts in the present wave of storytelling was Betsy's 'Tacketty Boots', about a man who didn't know any stories until one night he floated across the loch in an old boat and turned into a woman for seven years.

I wonder if there could be a deeper symbolism behind this tale than meets the eye? On the surface, it's the sheer preposterousness of the young man's experience of womanhood and wifehood that at last gives him a tale to tell. But looking at printed collections of stories, it often turns out that the key person from whom they were collected was a woman. The Brothers Grimm paid tribute to a woman near Kassell who gave them some of their best stories, recalling that 'Her memory kept a firm grip on all the sagas. She herself knew that this gift was not given to everyone...She told the stories thoughtfully, accurately, with wonderful vividness, and evidently had delight in doing it.' Laurens van der Post, who spent years collecting and subsequently telling the stories told to him by the Bushmen of the Kalahari desert, was first inspired to this interest by stories he heard as a child from his Bushman nurse, Klara. Duncan Williamson, who has filled many books with stories collected over a lifetime on the road, got his first inspiration from his grandmother who, so she told her grandchildren, kept her stories in a 'pocket' attached to a belt round her waist.

The Irish poet Padraic Colum, introducing the classic 1944 edition of *The Complete Grimms Fairy Tales*, wrote from his memories of childhood in rural Ireland how the storyteller's art reflected 'the rhythm of the night'; how, when it grew dark in the days before electricity, 'a rhythm that was compulsive, fitted to daily tasks, waned, and a rhythm that was acquiescent, fitted to wishes, took its place'. This 'rhythm of the night' would set a mood without which the traditional story would have diminished appeal. Interesting how, in a contemporary world whose nights are bright and bustling with electricity, those of us who feel drawn to tell stories instinctively light candles and bring in musical instruments that will draw the listening ear to a point of stillness before a story begins.

So it was that the travelling people with their fires and their poverty kept the stories going while the rest of the world got off on bright movies and loud pop music and, eventually, household television. All this is changing today. Most of the old Scottish traveller families now live in houses and own televisions – but those who still hold their oral inheritance of stories and songs have been generously passing them on to the rest of us, creating a new generation of storytellers and singers. Storytelling has something in common with the green movement – growing numbers of people choosing to withdraw from the grip of an entertainment industry in which most of us can only be consumers, turning to an art form that can only exist in a real space between people. And it is remarkably media-proof: film it or record it and its essential quality is lost.

It is a basic fact that a storyteller's voice needs to be *heard*. This was a problem for me in the beginning, coming from a quiet place behind a typewriter, as it can be to a lot of people from non-performance backgrounds. After I started running workshops and monthly performance evenings at Watermans Arts Centre in Bedford in 1985, I began to suffer severe bouts of laryngitis. People sitting at the back complained that they couldn't hear me. My doctor prescribed periods of total silence and my husband, a psychoanalyst, made a few interpretations to the effect that I didn't really want to be a storyteller. I rescued myself with Frankie Armstrong's help, discovering in her workshops that I could make as much noise as I wanted with my voice so long as I kept my throat open and relaxed and used my breath freely, letting it resonate through my entire body. I enjoyed singing and 'hoeing' imaginary fields, releasing an amazing volume of vocal power and recognising how tight and restricted my voice had been before. Finding my voice as a storyteller was the beginning of a process which, I now feel, has put me back in touch with a whole range of expressivity I had lost in childhood after separation from my parents in Brazil to be educated in an English boarding school. I brought Frankie's voice exercises straight back to my storytelling groups, passing on my discoveries and enjoying the opportunity to practise them over again with my friends. I have always done this, admitting unashamedly that when I 'teach' storytelling I am also learning as I go. Frankie's methods had a wonderfully liberating effect on the group and on people's expressivity in their storytelling, so that our gains were more than vocal. It was living proof that the expression 'finding a voice' has metaphorical as well as literal implications.

Over time, however, I came to recognise that I still needed something more than Frankie could give me if I was to understand and apply vocal work to the specific act of telling stories, working with the spoken as compared with the singing voice. I did some work with Margaret Leona, a Kew storyteller who had performed and taught voice before the war. This helped me with projection, but I still had a vague sense of needing to connect inwards with the breath, a sense that there could be a way of letting sound come from the very centre of me, which I could feel but not articulate.

Then I read a newspaper article about Cicely Berry's work with actors at the Royal Shakespeare Company. The headline was 'One from the Heart and One from the Ribs'. I was intrigued with this reference to 'the heart': I knew from experience that when my heart was touched by the *feeling* behind the words, this could release a vocal quality which brought things alive. I didn't know how I was going to get there, but I felt that I needed to work with Cicely. Somehow I managed to meet her after a platform performance at the Cottesloe (National Theatre) and said I was a storyteller and wanted to work with her. She was kind enough to invite me to join a weekend workshop with some drama teachers at Stratford.

That weekend with Cicely and her assistant Andrew Wade at Stratford was exciting. There was a full-bodied physicality and sense of fun that reminded me of Frankie's work. At the same time I was surprised and moved by the experience of embodying and resonating physically and emotionally with the language of Shakespeare, which I have always loved. At last I began to discover how the physicality of the voice can be brought to meet the feeling behind language. The breath is the key. These are my own words as I try to convey an experience that is almost impossible to verbalise. The use of the voice as an instrument is something actors learn which is of crucial importance to storytellers. For the record, it was lying on my back on the floor and working with the silent 'h' that gave me the inward connection I had been trying to find. But I got a great deal more than this from the workshop and a subsequent weekend with Cicely and Andrew at the Barbican. I have brought Cicely's techniques into my workshops, where I frequently have people leaping on and off chairs, playing with vowels, consonants and whispered lines, experiencing the energy and resonance of language.

Talking all this through with Frankie, I have come to realise that what most of us need for our voices is a kind of remedial work. We are born with good voices, but our capacity to use them can become stunted through the lives we lead. How many people spend most of their days seated in front of computer screens with only their fingers moving? Is it any wonder that we find our voices restricted when we come to tell a story or sing a song?

If we go back to the storytellers of Padraic Colum's rural Ireland, these were men and women who worked in a very physical way during the daytime. When they settled to the rhythm of the night, this physicality would have given a natural power and resonance to their voices. The same is true of storytellers in the traveller tradition. Their lifestyle is very different from the sedentary one I have just described. The young people still gravitate towards physical work, wanting to keep their bodies strong and their minds free. My friend Sheila Stewart, a magnificent ballad singer and storyteller, has a physical strength built on years of picking berries, digging turnips and lifting potatoes. I remember watching Sheila as she told a story of a young man who attacks Death when he meets him walking along the shore to get his mother 'and he battered him, and he battered him'. As she brought her fist down again and again, matching the action to the words, the strength of the movement was reflected in her expressive voice. And I thought 'There's a woman who has worked on the land. She knows how to hit things! Death wouldn't have stood a chance!'

Some time after I had worked with Frankie and Cicely, I was intrigued to hear that Sheila Stewart was planning to run a workshop she had devised as an attempt to teach something she called 'the Conyach'. 'What is it?' I asked and she replied 'It's what makes a traveller's voice send a shiver down your spine when you hear us sing.' I knew what she meant. A story or a song from a traveller can thrill you to the marrow with fear or sorrow, excitement or joy: the sound seems to go right into you. I have heard Sheila sing a ballad that begins 'False, false hae you been to me my love' and felt that shiver, something between excitement and fear, in response to an indescribable quality in her voice. I joined the workshop full of curiosity.

Sheila had devised a series of exercises which had us physically enacting a series of very graphic images. One had us holding on to angry feelings while she tried to pull them out of us: I was reminded of Cicely Berry using physical energy to help people get in touch with what she calls 'the aggressiveness of language'. Another of Sheila's exercises had to do with making a physical connection between voice, heart and soul. She wanted us to experience this connection as a physical fact and produce a vocal sound out of the experience. It was her way of sharing with us a connection she is aware of making within herself when she sings a ballad that moves her deeply.

Here was someone at a far remove from the research that informs the teaching of voice in places like the RSC, one woman from a family in which the singing of ballads is dying out, doing all she could to pass on her art to a new group of people who want to keep it alive. The workshop left me with a sense of having touched base with something very important, both in connection with Sheila and with my own inner world – of having made more solid the ground I stand on when I tell a story. This kind of personal connection has always been vital in the oral tradition. Again I remember Forster and 'only connect'. Perhaps this is the most important single thing we can do as storytellers.

For myself, the move from writing to telling stories, using my voice in place of a typewriter, opened up the way to a completely different kind of life. From working with storytelling groups I went on to train as a drama and movement therapist and thence into psychotherapy, exploring in depth some of the changes that I had first noticed through the telling of traditional tales. As a member of a drama therapy team working with emotionally disturbed children, using stories as a basis for regular session work, I have been astonished at the way these children could make deep and healing connections with us through the symbolic language of the stories. I have witnessed a child who had been chaotic and withdrawn arriving with the announcement 'I've got a story today' and then telling a well constructed tale built around traditional motifs, which we were then able to use for the basis of a drama session. This kind of breakthrough would sometimes coincide with a sudden coming together of the child's capacity to cope with academic work. There is something about the shape as well as the sound of stories that seems to pull us all towards wholeness.

Bibliography

Forster, EM, *Howards End*, Penguin, London, 1936
The Complete Grimms Fairy Tales, Pantheon, London,

1944; Routledge and Kegan Paul, London, 1975

Hopkins, Gerard Manley, 'God's Grandeur', *Poems and Prose*, Penguin, London, 1975

McGlashen, Alan, *The Savage and Beautiful Country*, Daimon, Einsiedeln, Switzerland, 1988

Sawyer, Ruth, *The Way of the Storyteller*, Bodley Head, Oxford, 1942

van der Post, Laurens, *The Heart of the Hunter*, Penguin, London, 1967

Whyte, Betsy, *The Yellow on the Broom*, Futura, London and Sydney, 1979

Williamson, Duncan, *Fireside Tales of the Traveller Children*, Cannongate, Edinburgh, 1983

Sound Advice
Women and Storytelling from India

Vayu Naidu

Spaces where stories are told act as voiceboxes for the totality of the story to happen. The human body is an instrument that contains the precious filament of voice which creates an arc of sound between the teller's and the listener's imagination.

In sanskrit aesthetics the word 'sahrdya' refers to a bridge of sound. It is a bridge that creates a rainbow of 'rasa' or emotions and moods that forms an arc between the teller and listener. The teller pours out a story. The totality of that story rests on a mosaic of elements that the storyteller combines with imagery, and gesture while focusing on tone and voice to set the mood. All these elements exist in the listener. The teller's function is to call out these emotions by means of a story, and the listener's function is to respond to the wisdom of the story by identifying with the emotions in it. The storyteller and listener have a strong partnership; the craft of storytelling is one of making co-respondences.

This essay attempts to show how this bridge of sound is built. I will look at some salient aspects of training that can set free the imagination and voice of the teller, from a socio-cultural perspective of stories told by women from India.

As a practitioner of storytelling, I have always rooted myself in the 'rasa', or emotional and geographical land-scape, of the story I choose to tell. The colours of the earth and sky, the foliage or rocks, the burning or warmth of the sun, lightness and heaviness of peoples' clothes, the muddiness or clear swirling pools, the sounds of washing, or lowing of grazing animals, and the cacophony of birds before they rest at night – all populate my visual reservoir of narrative imagery. Lying close to the skin of all these subtle and vibrant images is an unseen presence. It undulates with the landscape in the imagination, evoking 'reflection' from tawny sunsets, 'loss' from a cart and its driver moving away from its village, 'love' on seeing a woman with outstretched arms saluting the moon, 'anger' spiralling from a warrior who has been rejected at a tournament because of his low caste. This emotional consciousness that is evoked by images brings about an identification with the story on the part of the teller and a capacity for vivid imagining in the listener.

There are, of course, many more images and their companion emotions that strike a chord of association and identification between teller and listener. In India where I was born, spent my childhood, studied and grew into a woman, there are twenty-two states or regions with a heritage of languages and dialects. I have lived in ten of these states across north, west, east, central and south India. Each region and its diverse myths of origin, customs, cuisine and clothes is amorphously united by two epics, *Ramayana* and *Mahabharata.* The emotions of the epic are determined by the circumstances that the characters are in, and these have an accompanying terrain, season and time of day. So, geographical observation offers my narrative imagery a construct, and it is this rootedness in landscape that articulates the idiom of the region from where the story originates, while the telling is in English.

Emotional consciousness is codified in sanskrit aesthetics into nine basic emotions or 'rasa'. It is emotions that help the teller and listener to meet halfway on the bridge of sound. It is emotions that give expression to voice, and it is the voice that articulates the half-hidden truth about stories. All the factors work in a circular motion in a continuous cycle.

Now, technique and inspiration are so integrated that one has almost forgotten the process. What I clearly remember from my childhood as I recollect stories told by my grandmother in Telegu, the language of my first home, was the ritual oil bath on Saturdays. You lay down on a cane mat in the sun at about 8.30 in the morning, and warmed coconut oil was massaged into your body and poured into your hair. As the stretching and snapping of knuckles increased with the tempo of the oil bath, a story was poured, as it were, into your ear. The selection of story was dependent on your age and sex. The story of Savithri, which I am going to tell, has relevance to three lives, or stages, in the development of a listener: it could be told for a girl (to emulate quick wittedness), for a woman (to emulate being a steadfast wife), and here I am placing a feminist perspective – in enabling the listener to see how patriarchy dominates through symbols of finalty and power that can be broken to empower women. Traditionally, the third stage could have been for an older woman retelling the tale with the wisdom of experience and a fuller understanding of how social conventions operate.

Savithri was discovered, adopted and named by her royal parents after the guardian goddess Savitur. Alcestis, the heroine of Euripedes' play, is sometimes considered to be her European counterpart for her courage and persistence in bringing the dead back to life. When Savithri is old enough to be married, she tells her father the king that she does not want the conventional practice of 'swayamvara' or tournament. The 'swayamvara' offered an opportunity for princes to exhibit their valour: the one who captivated the princess's heart by his display of intellectual and physical prowess was garlanded and the marriage to the princess took place.

Instead, Savithri undertakes a journey in the forest with her old storyteller. A month passes and then, while returning to her father's kingdom, she crosses a stream with a very swift current. The old storyteller is unable to cross the stream with Savithri's nimbleness and slips into the swirling water, with her gnarled wooden staff. In a flash, a young man appears from the trees and saves the old woman by carrying her safely across to the bank. Savithri is first alarmed, then comforted by the compassion of the dazzling young man. Her heart is made captive by his prowess and humility. Names are exchanged, and Savithri returns to tell her father that it is Satyavan, the woodcutter she met in the forest, whom she will marry. The king tries to dissuade her but she is insistent.

To create a tighter twist to the knotted plot, Narada, the divine storyteller, is on one of his many visits to the court of mortals, and on hearing the news informs the royals that Satyavan is also a prince, but through the influence of his father's enemies, he and his blind parents have been exiled to live in the forest. The king is pleased that his daughter has chosen a partner of her class. But Narada goes on to say that Satyavan has a curse from a previous birth. In this life, if he marries, he will leave his bride a widow after 12 months. Savithri is still determined to marry Satyavan in spite of her father's warning:

Death is the only truth, and the truth is death;
a widow cannot remarry.

After their marriage, Savithri and Satyavan return to the forest with his parents. Here Savithri discovers the world of nature, in strong contrast to the manicured palace gardens of her father's kingdom, which she had loved with no awareness of a world beyond. As each day passes, she alone carries the burden of knowledge about Satyavan's imminent end. Each day as they grow closer, the foreboding doom grows heavier.

Towards the end of the eleventh month she decides to go on a fast for three days. Neither a sip of water nor a morsel of food passes her lips. At last she is able to see through to the spirit world. On the day of the twelfth month she agrees to go with Satyavan into the forest. He is radiant with Savithri beside him, and seating her on a grassy bank he leaves to chop wood. She hears the powerful blow of his axe and then sees him returning holding his head. Sinking onto his knees beside her, he dies with his head in her lap.

As Savithri now has a unique power to access the spirit world, she soon hears Yama, the God of death, riding his water buffalo singing:

Death is the only truth, and the truth is death;
A widow cannot remarry.

She is able to persuade him to let her follow her husband's body to the kingdom of death. Yama is impressed by her devotion and grants her three boons, each at different stages of the journey, but of course the clause is that she must not ask for her husband's life back. The first two boons are granted with wishes for the return of Satyavan's parents' kingdom and eyesight, respectively. The final boon she asks for is that her children and grandchildren may eat comfortably off a large gold plate. When this is 'granted' by Yama and she does not budge from her position as the boon is granted, she is able to quote him back saying: 'If a widow cannot remarry, how will I have children and grandchildren? And if children out of wedlock are not considered legitimate by any society, then to save my honour and that of all women it is best I have my husband's life back.' Of course Yama, with all the rules he made about being the upholder of truth, could hardly disagree.

The message of the story within the domestic milieu was straightforward. Trust your intuition, accommodate your husband's status whether it is comfortable or impoverished, with faithfulness, perseverance, constancy, and presence of mind. These were the ideals for young girls to emulate for their own marriage, as it was considered a necessary condition to life by elders even in my childhood.

I felt compelled to tell you a story in relation to its socio-cultural significance and my retelling has feminist under-tones of the struggles my generation encountered in India.

At the beginning of this essay I indicated that in sanskrit aesthetics there are nine rasas or states of emotional consciousness. These are:

love	anger
fear	heroism
laughter	disgust
grief	wonder
peace	

For the performer, each rasa has myriad combinations in terms of relationships, status, existential and cosmo-logical events. Each rasa can also be accompanied by a mood reflected by a time of day. Savithri's discovery is at sunrise. It is the time of day that possesses an auspicious nature. Savithri meets Satyavan in the late afternoon, when nature's calls for homecoming are in the air. Savithri has found the companion who puts her heart to flight, and rest. The royal family realises their predicament at night which has a foreboding quality to it.

Savithri meets Yama at noon, when there is a deathly silence all around, and finally has Satyavan returned to her at sunset, which has to do with new beginnings.

Now that life itself has spun another yarn, I am interested in bringing the reader's attention to a particular voice. Apart from the sociocultural motives that Grandmother had for weaving the tale, there is a very strong factor that resonates deep into my present, a time that is way after her death. It is not a personal or sentimental factor but what I call the metaphoric voice. This is the voice that carries with it the emotional expression and range of characters. It is an amalgam of internalising the story by identifying it with the teller's fantasies and life experience and tapping into a code of Indian musical systems which enables an improvised rendering of a story from the canon of received texts. Following years of research with women who tell stories in performance and professionally, I am now able to piece together the mosaic of Grandmother's own training, although she would never have been allowed, or even dared, to become a professional storyteller because of her caste and class. The streams of professional and domestic tellings are distinctive, and while the same repertoire of stories may be shared, the ways of telling them are different in terms of scale. In my discussion of training the voice below I will be illustrating the preparation of the voice common to both streams of storytelling, but evidently varying in intensity.

Each storyteller trains by waking in the morning and chanting. These 'slokas' or sanskrit verses are preceded with deep inhalation and exhalation exercises. On the exhalation the word 'Om' is uttered until the lungs are empty. These are done in various cycles of bass, tenor and alto resonating in the chest, nose and lips. The slokas are a concentration exercise with deep devotional associations. The sanskrit words create a range of syllabic and vocal exercises which make the tongue flexible, while also toning the cheek muscles.

Most storytellers in India have had musical training. Practising the scales are important. The openings of stories are important. The musicality of the voice, even if the entire narrative is spoken, is dependent on an inviting opening. Depending on the predominant rasa of the story, if it is 'courage' the voice of the storyteller takes on a commanding bass, which then modulates with the moods within the story.

The cycles of Om are important in understanding the significance of pauses, which are assisted by the complete exhalation of air and the space to inhale. It is the space between one Om, including its breaths, that is punctuated with silence. It is in this silence that the sound resonates in the body and forms a listening memory. Silences within the narrative make the listener listen more attentively, and the breathing helps the pace of the narrative. There are several breathing exercises that develop the stamina to perform a story without interruption of drinking water; 90 minutes or more.

One of the great devices for annunciating and diction is the counting of rhythms. A basic system of rhythm known as taal in Indian music is teen taal or three claps within a 16-beat cycle. This is considered the closest to natural rhythms in terms of pace in speech. Within one cycle of 16-beats a sentence can be delivered with one breath by the teller, and has clarity for the listener. Then there are half beats, slower or faster within the cycle, that can be used to pace the narrative accordingly to reflect the significance of the passage. I have been very lucky as a practitioner in England to work with Sarvar Sabri, who is a master percussionist on the tabla. We have successfully explored the possibilities of narrative and percussive rhythms in performance, at times working against the mood of the story and sometimes punctuating it.

In all musical systems in India, apart from the scales, there are vocal syllables or 'bol' that are learnt by pupils to ascertain the distinctive notes on the two hide-stretched sides of percussive instruments. This is correspondingly taught to dance students of both Kathak and Bharatha Natyam in their respective North Indian Hindustani and South Indian Carnatic vocabularies. In recent productions such as *Kathasuniasceal: Shape-shifting stories from India, Ireland and Africa* (1996–97) (Brumhalata Intercultural Storytelling Company), Indian syllables and rhythms were integrated with those of Yoruba as well as melodies from the Irish. This was a devised intercultural production that I had produced experimenting with this. In *The Ones who Dared* (1998) a Kathak dancer, Sonia Kundi Sabri, and a saxophonist, Jesse Bannister, were introduced and the production opened with syllables orchestrated by Sabri. The cadence and moods reflected in these, created a new language, while it was a skilful warm-up before entering the dimension of sound, word and movement and then music embracing all these in a complete intercultural storytelling performance.

In one of the stories about a young woman who takes a snake on as her mother there is a refrain about her afflictions from her marital home. Sonia, the dancer accomplished in her vocal syllables, repeats:

Dha na dha na dha na dha
dhi kita dhi kita dhi kita dha
dha na dha na dha
dhi kita dhi kita dha
dha na dha
dhi kita dha
dha na
dhi kita
dha

When this is accompanied with gesture it signifies the rocky path she has travelled and the varying intensity of her afflictions at her marital home.

I tell stories for their deep meaning. But what continues to fascinate me is the sheer sound of the word to match the image in my heart. Pacing and silences are integral to creating the significance of the story. I revel in sound – traffic, vendors, machinery, everything that is part of our urban and rural global landscape. To shape a language to convey the buzz, frustration, and mobility of these contemporary sounds within stories of older worlds is the challenge to bridge the world of the heart with the world of the eye.

I have forged a passage from being a listener and then a performer. Many of the voice rituals I have written about are part of the daily devotions, but for those in the profession it takes a considerably longer practice time. The metaphoric voice seems to be the first nerve centre that is touched in the storyteller's impetus to learn a story. It is the metaphoric voice that makes an intuitive leap between teller and listener which builds the bridge of sound. The physical voice is trained to contain the passage of emotions so that these can be manifested with sincerity, virtuosity and clarity. The external space of a room is integrated with the body which is the inner space pouring out an arc of images and emotions by means of the voice. The embodied voice transports the teller and listener into a realm that is there, deep within ourselves.

Bibliography

Ghosh, Manmohan, *The Natyasastra*, Royal Asiatic Society of Bengal, Calcutta, 1950

Deutsch, Eliot, 'Reflections on some aspects of the theory of Rasa', in Rachel Van M Baumer and James R Brandon (eds), *Sanskrit Drama in Performance*, University Press of Hawaii, Honolulu, 1981

Naidu, Alarmelu Mangathai Calpakam, oral rendering of *Savithri* in Telegu

Naidu, Vyjanthi, 'Tellers and Tales' in *Ramayana and Mahabharata: Contemporary theatrical experiments in English with Indic oral traditions of storytelling*, Ph.D thesis, University of Leeds, 1994

And Deep Things Are Song ...

Nóirín Ní Riain

And deep things are song. It seems somehow the very central essence of us, song; as if all the rest were but trappings and hulls.

Thomas Carlyle (1796–1881),
Scottish essayist and historian

Dreaming a song into being makes perfect sense for me of the essence of life. My entire journey to this moment has been bathed in song – sometimes lulled to rest in a near-perfect note, sometimes dropped deep into the wellspring of soundless despair only to angrily question the source and existence of that same note. It is from the balance between both of these worlds that my own story of singing shoots out and blossoms. It is this very experience that I will try to verbalise now.

This is one woman's truthful articulation of the power of the song. Inherited power, firstly, as we historically talk through some work songs and songs of desire from the Irish tradition that have moved me most. Secondly, as a singer within this tradition, I will try to articulate the experience of performance itself, with reference to the nine sister-goddess Muses and ensuing transcendence and transformation that sometimes happens. Thirdly, I want to think about my experience as listener and observer to many vocal traditions. These three interactive roles all hold a constant fascination for me, so I welcome this opportunity to share the elusiveness of this sound-butterfly which bewitches the singer, the song and the sung-to.

How a person sings and what a person sings both reveal the essence of the person. Therefore, understanding the voice is important on the deepest level of universal culture. There is a sense of being at the centre, at the nub of things – the throbbing heart of the bird, as it were. In this place we look to the past, first and foremost, for the guidance and courage that are part of tradition. And then, fortified by this confidence, knowledge and reverence for what has been the voice of our foreparents, we can face the future with self-assurance.

Donal O Sullivan (1893–1973), the Irish music historian, has written that 'Anyone who wants to know the mind and the soul of the Irish people must have recourse to their songs'. In any area of life, archaeological artefacts play a vital role in helping us to live with the past and in the present. But when it comes to imagining and recreating the deepest sounds of our foremothers and forefathers, something else is triggered off: a whole unexplored discography of the imagination and soul is unleashed. Anthropologists agree that every people has a song, a music which is the very essence of its society and cultural being. From the cradle to the grave, song enveloped the worlds of our foreparents. It is to this song repertoire from the Irish tradition that I now turn, looking primarily at those songs which were sung by women.

Every culture has its songs of work. As the West African proverb says, 'Without a song, the bush knife is dull'. Within the home, singing was an integral part of a domestic chore performed by most women – that of child-rearing. The Irish tradition unfurls a wonderfully rich, multi-coloured tapestry of child-directed song. On the one hand, there are the dandling songs created to distract and amuse the little one while awake. On the other hand, there are the lullabies – soft, soothing songs that bring 'sweet sleep down from the blissful skies'.[1] Both of these song types appropriately reflect these two strands of mothering in two very distinct styles: dandling songs are metrical and play on nonsense vocables, centring on consonants, such as *digeas o deamhas*, or *cucanandy*, while vowel sounds – *s'óabháin, seoith'n seó, lú, ló, ló* – over non-metrical vocal lines are characteristic of the lullaby.[2] Here is a verse of a Connemara dandling song which may contain some veiled desire, familiar at some stage to every mother, for some momentary relief of duty!

> *Caithim's suas is suas é,*
> *Caithim's suas an páiste*
> *Caithim's suas is suas is suas*
> *Is tiocfaidh sé anuas amáireach!*

> (We will throw him up and up,
> we will throw him up the baby,
> we will throw him up and up
> and he will come down tomorrow!)

Songs addressed to children, too, were for the most part solitary communications. Private song secrets passed between mother and child and were much more than just simple, uncomplicated ditties. Not only in Ireland, but all over the world, these songs are often cloaked bribes to the little one to be good and to go to sleep. Sometimes the promise is benign, though it may be unrealistic and fanciful: in Greece, a sugar city is promised; in France, a white bird that will lay a special egg; in Denmark, a mother pledges new shoes with shining buckles to her infant. Sometimes, however, the promise is dark and takes the form of fearful threats to little crying ones: German tradition says that a black and white sheep will come to bite the toes of the crying baby; in Spain, the crying one will be eaten by a black man. This traditional English baby-song[3] leaves no fragment of unfeeling imagination unturned!

Baby, baby, naughty baby,
Hush you squalling thing, I say.
Peace this moment, peace, or maybe
Bonaparte will pass this way.

Baby, baby, he's a giant,
Tall and black as Rouen steeple,
And he breakfasts, dines, rely on't
Every day on naughty people.

Baby, baby, if he hears you,
As he gallops past the house,
Limb from limb at once he'll tear you
Just as pussy tears a mouse.

And he'll beat you, beat you, beat you,
And he'll beat you all to pap,
And he'll eat you, eat you, eat you,
Every morsel snap, snap, snap.

The Irish tradition has a beautiful repertoire of other work songs, sung to accompany spinning, weaving and herding, 'to lighten the labour into an amusement by the singing of cheerful songs'.[4] These are songs to be shared with others – social singing as opposed to the rather solitary nature of mothering songs sung within the home. The whirring sound of the spinning wheel is enmeshed in the hauntingly magical vocables and jaunting rhythms within, for example, *s'ambó éara, bhuileabó éara* and *Ailiú Éana', áil'u éara'*.[5]

The largest repertoire of women's songs in Ireland is created by women's desires: songs of love unrequited, maternal love unfulfilled and loveless relationships (because of matchmaking) abound – indeed, songs expressing sheer happiness and contentment in love are rare. Tension, conflicts of desire and unrealised dreams were an essential inspiration for song. An excessive obsession with oneself, a necessary narcissism, marks the

Irish woman's voice, though this is also the typical response of the love-stricken woman throughout Europe.[6] Grief and disappointment in love, of whatever kind, ultimately culminate in a hidden spiritual wisdom that connects human relationship with that of the divine. A classic *sean-nós*[7] mid-eighteenth century song of unrequited love, 'Dónal Óg', gives majestic and noble expression to this connection between human and divine experience. The final verse ends despondently –

> You've taken east and west from me,
> You've taken my future and my past from me,
> You've taken the sun and the moon from me,
> And my greatest fear is that you've taken God
>   from me.

The eighteenth and nineteenth centuries, when much of the extant *sean-nós* tradition emerged, were a time of huge social change for women in Ireland which greatly reduced the number of songs surviving from this period. The growth of towns in the eighteenth century began a shift from ruralisation to urbanisation. Social life and religion began to move from the hearth to the town. In the last decades of the eighteenth century population growth meant that the primary preoccupation of thousands of Irish women became finding the means to feed their families. The Great Famine of 1845–1847 seems to have left the women of Ireland voiceless. George Petrie (1790–1866), the noted collector and antiquarian, remarked on the dirth of song airs '... now rarely or never to be heard because of ... the consequences of the calamities of recent years'.[8] But while the number of songs surviving from this period is greatly reduced, the songs that did survive reflect a unique stream of poetic and musical creative consciousness.

*

Religious song in Irish comprises three strands: eighteenth century religious poetry by known male poets, which was sung to popular airs of the time; religious poetry, which was deliberately wedded to unrelated, secular folk tunes by well-meaning editors for hymnals; and, finally, traditional spiritual songs which were collected, words and music together, from the one source. This latter stream represents the oldest, purist oral tradition.[9]

However, religion in eighteenth century Ireland was home-centred to an extent unparalleled among other Roman Catholic countries in Europe. The *rites de passages* of birth, death and marriage took place in the home, right into the middle of the nineteenth century, and there would always be music and song in these celebrations, with women involved as creators and singers. It is because religion was home-centred that no religious hymnology evolved organically in Ireland. But there is consequently this important body of traditional spiritual folk-song which has survived and shares a similar performance context with its secular counterpart. This *genre* of song has remained relatively untouched by change and is the oldest form of song to have survived in Ireland throughout the ages. These are songs that probe the depths of the soul and that resonate as loudly today as when they were first voiced.

How were these vocal gems – both sacred and secular – preserved and transmitted? Through archive recordings, through the living tradition of *sean-nós* singers, through manuscript and, in more recent times, through commercial recording. So through the very timbre and sheer uniqueness of this style, so different to either the popular or Western classical singing, is cherished and protected.[10]

There is an Irish proverb that says *Mo scéal fein – scéal gach duine*, meaning 'My story – everyone's story'. My own song-story is closely linked to the voices we have just briefly visited. My childhood memories are filled with snatches, not of *sean-nós*, but of popular parlour songs like

'The Old Bog Road', 'Somewhere over the Rainbow', 'My Grandfather's Clock' and 'O Danny Boy' – songs that I listened to every week of my youth when our extended family would gather together in our house, just before the advent of television in Ireland.

My voice for me as a little girl was a therapy, a comfort, a friend. As early as I can recall, I discovered for myself the experience Horace recorded 2000 years ago: *Minuentur atrae, Carmine curae* – 'Dark worries will be lessened by song'. Throughout a rather troubled, lonely childhood, I sang incessantly. I also prayed constantly. Song and singing expressed life, love, my very existence, for me – a medium of expression which was somehow linked to the heart of the Divine. My songs were 'off by heart' in the real sense. As a child, and now as an adult, spirituality – connecting with some space and place beyond the earthly experience – became, and increasingly becomes, stronger through chanting and singing. So it was that as a teenager, when I first heard 'Dónal Óg', the song of the young girl above addressing her young love, Dónal, that I identified strongly with her. Then and there my preoccupation and love affair with *sean-nós* were born! In *sean-nós*, particularly in the women's songs and spiritual songs, the perfect balance between the sacred and secular was maintained for me, both as a performer and as a listener. Wholeness, at-oneness, touched the same notes in my soul as Gregorian chant. Pure song, pure sound, pure ecstasy, pure music of the muses!

Music, singing and dancing appeal to a very fundamental need for expression in our very beings. Whether it is to participate directly as performer or to be part of the drama as a listener, there is something mythological woven into the very heart of music. Song and music at their source share something that defies definition, that has no basis in fact or natural explanation. Can one tangibly explain or define the perfect note that is the yearning of every singer?

The two words 'myth' and 'music' are both derived from Greek. Myth comes from the Greek *muthos*, meaning word, speech, tale or legend, the very essence of that which we know to be song. Every song tells its own tale, not just through word and speech but through the added layer of the language of music. Music, on the other hand, originated from *mousiké*, which refers 'to any art over which the Muses presided'. These nine sister-goddesses, the Muses, were daughters of Mnemosyne and Zeus – wild, mountain women from northern Greece, as I see them in my mind's eye when, as a singer of myriad song-moods, I am conscious of their spirits blessing and guiding the notes. Meet Clio, the muse of history, through the historical song; meet Erato, 'the lovely', as we sing or listen to erotic, passionate songs of desire. Polyhymnia is the inspirer of sublime hymns and serious sacred songs. Two of these goddesses traditionally preside directly over the singer: Calliope, meaning 'beautiful voiced', is the goddess of all singers: to voice her four-syllable name is a song in itself. Melpomene takes her name from the Greek *Mélpesthai*, which means 'to sing', but she is also the muse of tragedy. Thalia, or Thaelia, is the festive muse of comedy, of playful and idyllic poetry. Dancing and movement, choreology and choreography, are the domain of Terpsichore, a name that incorporates *choreia*. Euterpe, 'the well-pleasing', is the muse of lyric poetry, which is by its very nature song-like. Finally, Urania is the heavenly one – the goddess who connects the heavens and the earth, the sacred and the secular, in poetry, drama, dancing and song. On the male side, Apollo is joint patron of poetry, song and dancing and also the God of healing.

My fascination with the Muses and the whole mythological world of gods and goddesses and their connection with the voice goes back to a story that I read by the nineteenth century Scottish novelist and poet, George Macdonald. The quest of the singer for the ultimate entrance into 'the cavern where God weaveth the garment of souls' made perfect sense through this tale entitled 'The Parable of the Singer':[11]

> And lo! behind me was a great hole in the rock, narrow at the entrance but deep and wide within; and when I looked into it I shuddered, for I thought I saw far down the glimmer of a star. The youth entered and vanished. His guide strode back to his seat, and I lay in terror near the mouth of the vast cavern. When I looked up once more, I saw all the men leaning forward with head aside, as if listening intently to a far off sound. I likewise listened, but though much nearer than they I heard nothing. But I could see their faces change like waters in a windy and half-cloudy day. Sometimes though I heard nought it seemed to me as if one sighed or prayed beside me, and once I heard a clang of music, triumphant in hope; but I looked up and lo it was the listeners who stood on their feet and sang. They ceased, sat down, and listened as before. At last one approached me, and I ventured to question him. 'Sir,' I said, 'Wilt thou tell me what it means!' And he answered me thus. 'The youth desired to sing to the Immortals. It is a law with us that no one shall sing a song who cannot be the hero of his tale, who cannot live the song he sings, for what right hath he else to devise great things and to take holy deeds in his mouth. Therefore he enters the cavern where God weaveth the garment of souls, and there he lives in the form of his own dream, for God giveth them being that he may be tried. The sighs which thou didst hear were his longings after his own ideal, and thou didst hear him praying for the truth he beheld but could not reach. We sang because in his first battle, he strove well and overcame. We await the next.'

The names of the composers of women's traditional songs from the Irish tradition are, for the most part, unknown.

Songs present themselves completely disembodied and self-contained. What were these songwriters like? I find myself constantly asking, as their sung poems ring through my heart. Which is one of the reasons why I am fascinated with recreating the songs of the very first known woman composer in Western history – Hildegard of Bingen[12] (1098–1179), the Sybil of the Rhine, who declared that 'writing, hearing and knowing are all in one manner'.

There is an intimacy which one acquires through knowing, for example, that Hildegard was 42 years and 7 months old before she began to produce her massive output of writings, visions, the very first known morality play, and much more. Through these staggering literary achievements, we know her to be an ecologist, an apothecary, a herbalist, dramatist, visionary, cosmologist, prophet, preacher, singer and musician. Youngest of 10 children who suffered all of her life from a form of migraine, she lived to the ripe age of 81. She even created a secret language for her monastic daughters, a mysterious *Lingua ignota*, for the purpose of bonding them together.

During the 1150s, Hildegard eventually amassed the repertoire of songs, *Symphonia*, and completed the final version of her music drama, *Ordo Virtutem*, which comprises of her entire musical output. I have revelled in this repertoire for some 12 years now. What is extraordinary about this song collection is, in a nutshell, its highly imaginative and rhapsodic play with certain melodic patterns. Secondly, it shares with my own inherited *sean-nós* tradition and Gregorian chant all the freedom of oral composition and its innate, subtle rhythms. Pure inspiration and perfection from note to note, from hymn to hymn, something the twentieth century philosopher and novelist Iris Murdoch understood in her description of singing as '...the creation of sound by a disciplined exercise of mind and body...perhaps the point at which flesh and spirit most joyfully meet...the perfected cry of an individual soul'.[13]

As I draw to a close these personal musings on singing, the singer and the song, it is the feastday of St Benedict, Patron of Europe, 11 July 1999, and I recall his instruction 'And so sing the psalms that mind and voice may be in harmony'.[14] The central concept in all of this has to do with timing – timing that looks and listens back as far as one can see or hear to the Muses, to Hildegard, to the many anonymous voices of the Irish and Gregorian chant traditions. To hear and listen, as profoundly as at the moment of the birth of those sounds. It's almost as if time stands still in song and the voices and presences of the composers, whoever they were, and the line of singers since, are all around us. As a singer, I have felt this reaching out from them to us. Those writers and singers of the past are reaching out, helping out, joining in the chorus.

Looking ahead from this point in history, I think of Seamus Heaney's line about '...a music you would never have known to listen for'.[15] Timing again, and synchronistic, as we raise our voices to greet the new millennium. In the midst of world chaos and unrest, the singer will deliver the message of peace. Song will quell the nations. People of every nation will sing to and for one another. It is the time of new song epiphanies – to explore, expose and recreate new, and old, expressive ways of telling the world's song story. And everyone will sing!

> Everyone suddenly burst out singing
> And I was filled with such delight
> As prisoned birds must find freedom
> Winging wildly across the white
> Orchards and dark-green fields; on – on – and out of sight.
>
> Everyone's voice was suddenly lifted
> And beauty came like the setting sun.
> My heart was shaken with terror; on horror
> Drifted away...O but everyone

Was a bird; and the song was wordless; the singing will
never be done.

Siegfried Sassoon (1886–1967)

Notes

1. Alfred Lord Tennyson, 'The Lotus Eaters', The English Parnasus, OUP, London, 1961.
2. For a recording of this and other lullabies, hear *Celtic Soul*, Nóirín Ní Riain, Living Music, Connecticut, 1996.
3. Jean Harrowen, *Origins of Rhymes, Songs and Sayings*, London, 1977.
4. John O'Daly, *Poets and Poetry of Munster*, CP Meehan, n.p., 1888.
5. Recorded on Oro Damhnaigh, Gael Linn, 1979.
6. Evelyne Sullerot, *Women on Love*, The Chaucer Press, London, 1979.
7. Pronounced 'shan nos', it literally means 'old style' and is the Irish term for the entire genre of traditional song in Irish.
8. George Petrie, *Ancient Music of Ireland*, self-published Dublin, 1889.
9. Nóirín Ní Riain, 'The Nature and Classification of Traditional Religious Song in Irish', *Music and the Church*, Irish Academy Press, Dublin, 1995. Also Nóirín Ní Riain, my MA thesis 'The Music of Traditional Religious Song in Irish, University College, Cork, 1980.
10. For a classic recording of sean-nós, hear Deora Ailie CD, Claddagh Recordings CC6 with Maíre Áine Ní Dhonnacha. On that question of describing the timbre, Alan Lomax, the collector, states that correlations exist between a given society's sexual sanctions and its vocal style. In societies where premarital sexual activity is restricted, a high degree of 'narrowing and

nasality, both signs of tension, become prominent and constant features of a culture's singing style'.

11. George Macdonald, *Within and Without: a dramatic poem*, London, 1855.

12. Barbara Newman, *Sister of Wisdom: St Hildegard's Theology of the Feminine*, Scholar Press, Aldershot, 1987.

13. Iris Murdoch, *The Philosopher's Pupil*, Chatto & Windus, London, 1989.

14. Gerard MacGinty, *The Rule of St Benedict*, Chapter 19, Dominion Publications, Dublin, 1980.

15. Seamus Heaney, 'The Rain Stick', *The Spirit Level*, Faber & Faber, London, 1995.

The Healing Voice

Olivea Dewhurst-Maddock

Singing, when I was two years old, to my sick grandmother, is one of my earliest memories. I was trying desperately to keep my balance while standing on the steeply inward-sloping rush seat of a traditional Lancashire 'ladder-back' cottage chair. Remembering the tune and three verses of words at the same time, I already knew that the show – my little show – must go on! Singing has provided the continuity of my life and now, technically a pensioner, I love the art and craft and therapy of singing with a passion that increases with each passing year.

I knew from early in life that singing was more than virtuosity, more than entertainment, much more than career and 'success', but I met very few other musicians with whom I could speak freely of my ideas. It was only gradually that I found the confirmation of my dreams and the opportunities to practise and teach them. How wonderful that today we can write books like this book, attend conferences of sound therapists and have our researches discussed on radio, TV and the Internet.

So what is healing? What exactly do we mean by this frequently used word? Healing is the re-integration of the broken and separate parts of original wholeness. Healing can only begin with recognition of the broken-ness. Healing is the remembering of the fragments, of the original design. It is the recollection of the whole being in which each one of us has a part. Ultimate healing is when the part and the whole are one.

In this work of healing, the voice as healer and the nature of music are seen and heard as the manifestation of cosmic unity. Starting with the voice, I offer some thoughts for your consideration:

- Everything in creation, from the atom to the galaxy has a voice, ie all objects and all functions are possessed of a unique vibrational pattern, a specific, recognisable 'signature' of rhythmic and resonant being.
- Each human voice carries a unique pattern of individuality; no two voices are alike; there is a strand of sounds which only *my* voice and another which only *your* voice can contribute to the music of the world; that contribution is essential and irreplaceable.
- The voice is a true sound-mirror of being, a sonic 'barcode' of whatever we are, the sum of all our yesterdays and the promise of all our tomorrows.
- Voice is the interface between the inner world of thoughts, feelings, memories and dreams – and of their expression. It is the bridge between conscious and unconscious areas of experience.
- Importantly, the voice cannot lie. It carries truth and expresses what is authentic to us.

Voice, then, is the symbolic link between the archetypal idea and its expression. The function which distinguishes humanity within the spectrum of nature is not, as we tend to suppose, communication and language – all creatures have a measure of this, however little – but the capacity for symbolic communication. This is the sacred magic through which movement extends towards dance and ritual; verbal communication evolves into poetry; the need for shelter and safety produces architecture; observation and reflective thought are extended to produce mathematics, geometry, visual art and music.

Ancient cultures understood music as the creative energy through which forms are made. So the primal creative force is described in different cultures as the

Word, the Breath, Nada Brahman, the Song Maker etc. Within this order of creation, we are resonances of the original creative sound, endowed with the same potential. In this sense we are 'made in the image of God'.

Both ancient wisdom and recent research tell us that our habits of negative thinking and feeling can bring about change in our patterns of health; that destructive relationships can make us ill. In other words, it is possible for one part of our divided self to make war on the other part and, in the process, to dismember the whole person. This knowledge presents us with a continuous dilemma. All problems are gateways to learning, even if the learning curve is a steep one. With this particular problem it is important to know that we have the means to turn the situation round. Positive thought and loving feelings can heal, liberate and reconstruct the pattern of our being. In this way we can free the intelligence of the body to be whole, strong and beautiful and we can even develop a resistance to illness. Since energy follows thought, whatever we hold within our emotional inner world will eventually manifest through our cells and tissues, affecting the chemical reactions and metabolic processes of our physical being.

Harmony, balance and proportion are the essential qualities of musical sound. When we sing we immerse ourselves in these qualities, supplying our consciousness on a cellular level with the universal values and reassurance of participation in the symphony of life. The essential elements of music – rhythm, melody and harmony – provide us with a basic model for all healing processes.

So how do we join in? How do we negotiate a movement towards re-integration which will enable us to reconnect with our own deepest nature, enabling us to feel at home wherever we may find ourselves?

The first action required for this process to begin is to learn to listen, listening more and more deeply, listening to ourselves, to each other, to nature, to the planet. Through listening we gradually come to hear more and more. This enhanced listening begins by discovering silence – the many silences from which all sounds arise and to which all sounds return. Physical loss of hearing need not be a barrier to this process.

There is a lot of sound pollution in our environment. Noise, which is chaotic sound, is a serious source of mental and physical ill-health. It makes us long for the natural sounds of the sea-shore, the forest or the mountains. Freedom from chaotic noise is an important part of our precious holidays. At the same time there is a strange *fear* of silence when we are alone. We have the radio for company without really listening to what is said. We have musical wallpaper piped into shops, waiting rooms and even into our telephones. The more we grow to love silence, the more pleasure, understanding and healing we become able to receive from music.

The act of singing follows a sequence: each part of this sequence contains elements of wisdom and healing. The steps of the sequence are:

- *Breathing:* we can survive three weeks without food, three days without water, but only three minutes without air. Our life in this world begins with our first breath and our first vocalisation. Breath is the symbol of life.
- *Listening:* being open to life, giving ourselves attention, learning to recognise and value other voices, other lives, other selves.
- *Sounding:* uttering vocal sounds, giving soul and consciousness to the living spirit of the breath.
- *The vowel sound:* the quality of feeling, where sound and colour meet: sense beyond language.
- *Articulation:* the gathering of form, the garment of language; precision and definition.

All these functions serve the creative imagination and open the way for us to enter into our inheritance of communication through music and poetry, investing us with a commission to inspire, delight, comfort, bless and heal.

The following exercises were devised as steps towards the process I have just described.

Exercise 1a
Set aside a few moments each day for listening for the silences: pauses between words; spaces between the notes of music. Try to hear the silences as a visual artist learns to see the spaces around the objects of vision. The silences have a shape and a character of their own. Gradually, you will begin to sense them as realities. This exercise is the sonic equivalent to a 'detox' diet.

Exercise 1b
As with 1a, but this time listen deeply and lovingly to the sounds. Do not strive to analyse, assess, criticise or judge the sounds. Simply accept them, listen to them, listen *into* them and *through* them to the energy patterns they represent. There is an ocean of sounds around us, many and varied, most of them going unheard and unattended. After a time, listen to the sounds and the silence, seeking to feel the interaction between them. They are like a design set against a background – sometimes the sounds seem like the 'pattern', sometimes the silence. What is important is that they are equal in their meaning and value.

Exercise 2
Making *your own* sounds; loving and respecting your voice; giving undivided attention to its sounds and its silences. (Loving attention is one of the few things that is truly ours to give!) As your confidence grows, enter into a

musical relationship with the sounds around you: sing to the sea, to the plants in your garden, to the music of china tea-cups; sing your favourite songs, nursery rhymes, singing games, hymns and campfire songs with your friends. Listen with love to each other.

The first element of music is *rhythm*. In therapy, rhythm is a symbol of existence, of the life force itself, of energy, of willpower and endurance. All we can perceive of the cosmos is rhythmic. All creatures live by the pulse of nature that brought them into being. The seasons, the movements of the solar system, the persistent growth of crystals – all forms have a grounding in cyclical return. In health, the interlocking rhythms of cell and organ and function and renewal are strong and poised. Sickness is a-rhythmic. All the skills that you have mastered in life are characterised by the relaxed rhythm of integrated performance. Activities that have yet to be mastered feel, and give the impression of being cack-handed and maladroit. Rhythm restores our contact with vitality, with our own potential and with time (the result of our experience of movement in space). Rhythm releases the grip of an overactive intellect, the restrictions of cleverness and forced knowledge. It is a true obedience to life and to the divine seed core of our individuality. It is release from inertia and gives us the freedom to truly live.

Exercise 3
Bring your attention to the rhythm of your breathing. Do not seek to make it different. Do not count the breaths. Just breathe them. Allow your body to show you its rhythm: the rhythm will not be mechanically regular. Rejoice! You are not a machine. You are a living microcosm of the whole and all the rhythms of creation find their counterpart in you. Allow your heart to breathe: your emotional self; your busy, over-worked and under-used mind; your imagination; your unconscious self.

Breathe out love and breathe in new life. This exercise will help you to attune yourself to the rhythms within and around, rhythms of activity and rest, of giving and receiving. It will develop the awareness of unity with and trust in the order of the cosmos.

Exercise 4
Find your own heart-beat and listen to it with reverence. This is the basic pulse by which you *feel* all other rhythms. Upon this pulse you can build all the other patterns of movement. Experiment. Observe the rhythms of your walking, of your talking; how you carry out various tasks; how you gesticulate in animated conversation; how you dance. Use a tambourine or a drum – or your best instrument, your voice – to make patterns which complement your heart-beat. You will discover that fast, exciting rhythms will speed up your heart Slower, gentle patterns will slow it down in just the same way as a lullaby, timed to synchronise with the mother's heart and a rocking movemnt, will send a baby to sleep.

One specific frequency, a vibrational rate within the parameters of human hearing, if sustained for more than one sixteenth of a second, produces the auditory stimulus we experience as *pitch* – one note distinct from all others. A series of such notes results in a *melody*.

In healing, pitch is related to our sense of individuality and an awareness of where we are in our personal journey. Pitch provides us with an anchorage, a real sense of belonging, especially in childhood. Our ability to pitch notes accurately varies from day to day, according to the security of our self-knowledge. It empowers us to realise our own unique worth and to recall our individual pathway through the pilgrimage of a lifetime. Melody heals feelings of confusion, abandonment, loneliness and alienation. It overcomes antagonism and feelings of being unloved and unlovable and the terror of being left alone in the dark. It restores us to a sense of purpose and frees us to replace fear with love and trust.

Exercise 5
Sing any note that feels comfortable, not too low and not too high. Listen carefully. Pause for a few moments of silence and then see if you can recall the sound once more. See how far you can lengthen the pause without losing the original sound. Don't judge.

Exercise 6
Experiment with melody-making. Sing a tune using only two notes, then three, and so on. Have fun with this process: we learn most rapidly when we experience our lessons as *play*. Note: we *play* musical instruments, we don't work them.

After this exercise it will be easier to grasp any melody you want to sing: you will be aware of how it is constructed and how it grows – all by listening and singing.

Exercise 7
A continuation of Exercise 4 is to listen to the speech melody in a simple sentence, noticing the rise and fall of the words, and then try to translate that into singing. This teaches two things: (1) just how much musical content there is in spoken language and (2) how singing, as tuned speech, takes communication into another dimension.

Exercise 8
Singing with an 'anchor note', or drone. For this exercise, sing with a friend. Take turns to sing one long note (not forgetting to breathe!). The other partner makes a melody alongside continuing sound. You will be surprised how good this can sound and how inventive you really are. You will gain confidence in keeping your own sound and in

experiencing independence and co-operation together.

Harmony in music is the soul of sound longing to return to its source. In the voice, it is the inner disposition of the natural harmonics which give the vocal sound its integral tone, or *timbre*. In healing, harmony restores relationships. It is the force of unification, of bridge-building, of partnerships, of groups, of all who love.

Exercise 9
For this exercise you will need to share your experiment with a small group of friends. Make a circle – standing, sitting or lying down (all that matters is that you should be comfortable). Slowly and quietly begin to sing. Sing your own sounds, at the same time listening to each other with great sensitivity. Be patient and keep it simple. You will find that harmony will happen without any contrivance, because harmony is a natural part of our structure and instinct. Once you get going the dynamics can become more adventurous. One variation is to sit on the floor in a close group, facing outwards with backs touching. Sing just one chord of unplanned sounds and end together. Listen to the silence that follows. This can be quite a challenge and is always a profound musical meeting. It is a way to learn to be a stronger, more united group and, at the same time, a stronger, more relaxed individual.

Exercise 10
Stand with a partner, facing one another about 12 inches apart. One singer sounds a note at a comfortable pitch and the other sings a note which harmonises well, eg if we are in the western scale, a major third (the first two notes of 'While shepherds watched') or a perfect fifth (the first two notes of 'Twinkle, twinkle, little star'). Continue the two sounds as long as possible (not forgetting to breathe). You will feel yourself being magnetically drawn towards your partner, sometimes to the point of losing balance. A

supporting group will confirm that this is happening. This exercise proves to us the power of harmonising sounds to attract and unite and helps us to understand the extraordinary bonding that singing in harmony can create.

As your awareness and confidence grow you will discover and devise exercises for yourself and acquire insights of your own. Live and enjoy every step of the exploratory journey. Progress will be evidenced by your growing vitality, poise and ability to relax; by sounding without fear of your unfolding self; and by the realisation that harmony is more than a longed for, far off dream, but the truest nature of your being.

Bibliography

Dewhurst-Maddock, Olivea, *Healing with Sound*, Gaia Books, London, 1993

McClellan, Randall, *The Healing Forces of Music*, Amity House, Warwick, New York State, 1988

Garfield, Laeh M, *Sound Medicine*, Celestial Arts, Berkeley, California, 1987

Music to listen to

Bach, *Unaccompanied Violin Music*, Deutsche Gramophon 3371 030

—*Unaccompanied Cello Music*, HMV SL S 798

Barber, *Adagio for Strings*, Argo 2RG 845, distributed by Polygram

Williams, Vaughan, *Fantasia on a Theme of Thomas Tallis* and *The Lark Ascending*, Argo 2 RGC 15696

Language of the Heart, Voices of the Self

Michele George

> A twisted root straining to the light
> Shaped by stones and hard ground
> But keeping faith:
> Rest now in the nurturing womb
> Of the Dark Mother,
> Receive back
> Memories
> Of who you will become —
> And bud!

> Song created by a participant at a
> Belfast Voice Workshop, October 1999

My father died before I was born. I was four months in the belly of my mother, quite complete in all my parts. My mother, at the then ripe old age of 29, had married the man she loved just a year before he died. I asked her, in my adulthood, what she did and how she grieved back in the 1940s. She replied that of course she could not cry at home: the family would have been too upset. She had always been the pillar, acknowledged for her bravery and selflessness. So she kept up a strong front for the family and took the dog for walks in the park, to a private place where she would scream out her broken heart.

Thus I began my struggle with abandonment very early. Thus began my silencing, as I received in her womb, with complete vulnerability, the fullness of her denial on the one hand and her gut-wrenching wails of grief and loss on the other. She once let slip that she had raged against my growing whole inside her. Why was it him and not me who had to die?

We have all had our voices stolen from us. We have been silenced. It is not our fault.

I speak this knowledge to clients every day. I offer it to those who come for one to one voice work in my private practice. I insist upon it in my workshops and seminars, where people have agreed to work together and weave their voices with a multitude of others, all wounded and communally hopeful. I bring it forth at conferences where a thousand can rejoice together in the birthright of voices raised in song and in recognition of the storytellers we are all meant to be.

At a conference on Women's Spirituality in 1996, at the Washington National Cathedral, an exquisite edifice high on a hill in Washington DC and mainly the site of politically high-profile funerals, an unforgettable event took place. Women were invited to bring their under-standing, their hopes, their doubts, their fears and their every shape and form of spirituality. They brought their questions and their yearnings in profound ways. The organisers hoped for 300 women, which would cover expenses. Ten days before the event they cut off the registration at 1000: a thousand women from all over North America and Europe. There were many workshops, keynote addresses and intimate gatherings as people recognised each other on many levels. We sang a lot – in gratitude, in grief, in prayer and for the sheer fun of it. At the very end of the gathering we joined voices and as 1000 women strong sang 'Amazing Grace' the Gothic rafters vibrated in contentment and completion.

> Amazing grace, how sweet the sound
> That saved a soul like me...

Personally I have served my time as a 'wretch', the original word in the songwriter's needy verse. I now take the liberty to be a soul and to give voice from this central place in full embodiment. It is time for us to take these liberties and make them our own.

Everyone has a unique story. Over the years I have posed to thousands the question 'How were you silenced? How was your voice stolen?' There has always been a response: it could refer to a specific moment, a family configuration, a particular time span or perhaps a history of repeatedly moving home, having to begin again every year throughout the formative years of life. Everyone is aware that they have been shut up and shut down, but it is women who are responding in droves to this new awareness. Men do come along for help, but women seem to be more willing to take the risks in their awareness of the necessity to reclaim the voice as a recognition of their birthright, a necessity for survival. It is women who remember the ancestors, just as it is they who remember the birthdays and anniversaries. The birthright of voice is a lawful aspect of being feminine, something to be celebrated as we work to undo the bondage that has come to light in these transformed times in which we are now living.

As I continue with my own story I am led back once again to my mother's life and the fate that I shared as her daughter. Her name was Dorothy and she was a beautiful, highly intelligent woman with plans. She planned to go to university in order to become educated and free. In the 1930s this was not a given as it was for me in the 1960s. She was the eldest of an Irish-Catholic-American family living in Trenton, the capital of the state of New Jersey, a stone's throw from both New York City and Philadelphia. She had a sister two years younger than herself and then four brothers, all two years apart. When she was 18 years old her beloved mother dropped dead of a heart attack during a game of bridge. In that instant Dorothy's life was irrevocably transformed. Along with being abandoned and becoming a motherless child herself, she became mother to the five younger children and homemaker for her father. After my father's death she never remarried. Perhaps once the pain of mourning was over she came to enjoy a freedom from domestic ties which she had never known before. Being beautiful and witty and a lot of fun, she always had a boyfriend when I was growing up and I learnt early on to manipulate them to my own ends. Each boyfriend would stick around for a while until it became clear that she was not going to become his wife, then he would disappear and someone new and hopeful would take his place.

A visit to the previous generation deepens the inheritance. My mother's mother, Anna Doherty, was a baby in a crude cradle one day on a dock in Ireland in the late 1880s. Her family had scrimped and saved and were boarding ship for a better life in America. Getting from dock to ship was chaotic. Passengers and baggage had to be rowed out to the tide line and the Doherty family was large. When all were on board there was a head count and the littlest one was missing. Anna had been left on the dock! My great-grandmother became hysterical and a frantic search ensued. She was found and all was well, but was it?

My great-grandmother and her family were torn from all they knew, abandoning their home to survive the great hunger. What do we inherit? There is a consistency in the generations that preceded me: abandonment, loss and terror of loss abound; no father for me and too much father for my mother, placing me in the fourth generation of a line of strong women. This is but one story. Each story I hear is moving and every story must be told.

The stolen voice, the silenced voice, creates patterns that govern our lives. There is an extraordinary awakening as the realisation of this opens up the yearning to reclaim the voice as a birthright. Of course all this can be said of men as well: though the manner of telling is somewhat different, the depth of silencing is the same. But here we are specifically exploring the characteristic journey that women make as they move with tremendous courage to deny the 'invisibility' that has cloaked them for so long. It is fascinating to hear about this over and over: 'I cannot bear to be invisible any longer!' This will often be spoken in a tiny, wee voice, though it is sometimes boomed forth. It can be spoken through a huge smile or sobbed in full body spasm. Our cloaks of silence come in an astonishing array of colours, patterns and materials. Each story is utterly unique and yet the bodily response is remarkably similar, so it easily becomes communal. Thus we find a field in which to work.

When we observe a baby giving voice, we are astounded at the power contained in the tiny body of the child. We are born giving voice. It is truly a birthright and one of the few acts a human baby can perform on its own. Colts are up and running, deer are on their feet within hours. Babies of our species are born with a voice which can speak of need, of contentment, of primitive desire. We wait for that sound before declaring the child to 'be' *sound*, also to be breathing on its own, to be able to respond to the shocking mystery of its new environment outside the womb.

What happens when a baby cries? The preparation is all-encompassing. The body begins to fill, to fill with more and then with even more air. The belly is expanded to huge proportions. The limbs are extended as if reaching out. The face is in hungry movement. All is in readiness. There is a wonderful moment of complete stillness and then comes the great cry – total commitment to the vibration of the sound of the self. If this is indeed our right, if this is what we do so well, why does it go away?

Sound and creation are closely linked through recorded history. Explore the creation myths from around the world. There are many tales of the beginning of time which have us all emerging from the vibration of sound. Our own Judeo-Christian Bible is a prime example – in two versions, moreover: 'In the beginning was the Word, and the Word was with God, and the Word was God.'

I along with many others believe 'word' to be an inappropriate translation. I believe it refers more to that which is unique to the human being upon this planet – the ability to relate, to reach out with mind, heart, body and soul, all in the ineffable yearning to reunite with the divine source from which we all emerge. It is our unique ability to relate to one another that lays the foundation stones for this temple to be constructed, the temple which is the body, in which the work can be accomplished.

'And God said, "Let there be light." ' The Saying invokes the Light. The sound permits creation to burst forth in full illumination. Search around the world. This story is held sacred in countless cultures and kept alive in numerous traditions where storytelling flourishes. It stokes the fires of our humanity.

My work, which I call Re:Sound, grew out of the extraordinary circumstances of my professional life. I have been blessed to work with theatre luminaries such as Peter Brook and Joseph Chaikin, founder of the Open Theatre of New York. I have travelled the world with these and other seekers and a deeper knowing of the human voice has always been an urgent concern for each one, as it has been and continues to be for me. I have sung all my life – first in self-defence and with a very desperate need to be heard, evolving into the here and now, where living in my voice and voicing my life is my place of fearlessness in this world. My present mission is to extend this invitation to others and to bear witness and be a safe container as the work proceeds and the voice returns from disembodiment to home.

Ten years of analysis with the renowned Jungian analyst

Marion Woodman began three years after I arrived in Toronto in 1980. We were on a quest to rekindle the essence of storytelling and the stripping away of cultural and personal habits which limit us as to the vast choices we possess to bring the story to blazing life. We do indeed have to leave home in order to recognise that home is within. Marion is a firm believer in the power and reality of the body as home to the soul, which makes her a definite rebel in the Jungian world and offered me fertile ground in which to reap the potent seeds that had been sown in me over the years. We began to give workshops and seminars together. I worked with the voice, literal and metaphorical, while Marion worked along with the dreams of the participants. The link was undeniably present. My story must be told. Your story must be told and heard. Our music cannot remain locked away inside us or we will stop, wither and slowly extinguish the flame.

Clients are drawn to this work for an astonishing variety of reasons. The women who come have recognised their silencing, both as individuals and as a sisterhood. All are demanding a reclamation of the voice of their birthright. They tell their stories, each a unique jewel, and they weep for that which has been lost. It takes tremendous courage to choose to work with the voice. I never take it for granted. I humbly acknowledge the vulnerability which is being opened to scrutiny. When a woman shows up on my doorstep for the first appointment half an hour late I'll enquire if she got lost on the way, and she might tell me that this could be so. She has been walking up and down the street for that half an hour, looking for the courage to open the door. Women will ring up and tell me they have had my brochure in the car for a year now and, well, here we are – shall I come and see you? Women come because they long to sing again: they sang lullabies to their children until those children reached the necessary age of separation, which is no longer ritualised in our society. So often the child then humiliates the mother and shames her into singing no more, when thanks to her babies she has found a voice long stifled. Some come with highly developed singing voices, where the shame of the story which occurred so many years ago has restricted the glorious instrument to an audience of one and their theatre is the car.

I see many survivors of all natures of abuse -- sexual, emotional, physical. The blanked off silence that has shrouded the woman is profound. To have given voice could have been a literal death sentence. In such a case, her therapist will refer the woman to me when it becomes time to re-embody the vibration of the sound of the self. Disembodiment has been the only means to literal survival for so many for so long. The work then is gentle, patient and embracing. To breathe from the belly is to stir up the memories, and breath is at the heart of it all.

Looking at stories of vocal silencing, I often refer to the belly as the 'swamp'. A swamp is a very still place of great beauty and mystery. No birds sing there and yet there is a vibration which is compelling. If one throws a stone into a swamp, a movement occurs. This is the breath reaching down through muscles long held as armour. The stone creates ripples and the body responds. Throw another stone. A clear space of water appears and, with each successive stone, with each new embodied breath, the water begins to move once more. All the life that has been deeply unfolding becomes apparent. These forms are our unique creations – these two headed frogs, these three tailed snakes, strange water spiders and fish of a colour never before seen. The shadow is brought to life and the voice emerges. This is the stuff of creativity. This is what has been hidden for so long in fear that it would be seen and in terror that it would not. The sound that emerges may be a gentle, breathy sigh – a voice from deep within, no longer strangled in the throat, but travelling from the bottom of the well, vibrating the body again and at last.

The image of the well is a powerful one in Re:Sound work. I use as my logo the symbol of the Chalice Well at Glastonbury, a profoundly sacred site in England.

This symbol is on the cover of the well. The well is pouring forth endless quantities of water and has been for hundreds of years. This is the story I often tell:

> The well is your body. The well cover is lodged in your throat. It is there as a necessary protection and has been since you were small. We work together to remove the well cover, *not* to throw it away, but to hold it in the hand so that it is in your control. There are necessary times for the protection of the well cover. But you must make the choice now when it shall be on and when it shall open up to reveal the interior of the well. The ancient story goes that Joseph of Arimathea brought the chalice of Jesus Christ from Jerusalem after his death. This is the Holy Grail, kept deep in the well to hide it and protect it from harm. Glastonbury is a mixed site, just as are you and I. St Michael's Tor, a gently sloping hill and a potent piece of earth, is said to be where Avalon once was. It is here that Arthurian legend and Druid tales comingle: the Judeo-Christian and the pagan merge. This historical detail has relevance to the re-awakening of the voice in its full and true embodiment. We have lost touch with the pagan, by which I am referring to a sense of intimate relationship between

ourselves and Nature in all its aspects. The feminine Earth, the fertile body, requires vibration: it demands resonance for its health and evolution.

Let us say that the Grail is the human voice. Let us imagine that this Grail, this voice, is at the bottom of the well: it has been hidden there to keep it safe. Let us also imagine a dragon and perceive this dragon as the guardian of the Sacred Cup. Since she has been undisturbed for so long, she sleeps. Then the stones begin to drop through the swamp to the bottom of the well. The breath brings the voice down. The centre of gravity descends from the head and journeys to places long forgotten. The belly muscles act as bellows, bringing air fully into the lungs. The bellows stoke the fire and the voice finds its heat. Or, to put it another way, the dragon is awakened and breathes fire as its assigned task.

The movement thus created in the being of a woman stirred into this awareness requires scrupulous attention and care. The patterns are beginning to shift. Change is in the air and we do not always welcome change. This may be the moment when the first small song dares to emerge, the first deep groan is allowed its life. The first step is the most difficult, but there is joy waiting not too far along the path. Time is relative here. I worked with a client some time ago for about two years. Her story was heartbreaking and yet she came, week after week. For some months she would come in the door of my workspace, which is warm and inviting and a comfort to most. She would shut the door behind her, then sit right to the right of it on the floor, hands clasped around her knees. Sometimes an hour would pass in seeming silence, although breath is a powerful story to hear. I was in a chair across the room, by the window, where light would be streaming in. An empty chair was across from me – it was hers for the taking. Sometimes I would hum. One day she began to hum as well. A week later she came in, closed the door and sat to the left of the door, moving towards the light. Gradually she worked her way to the chair, finding small sounds – and some huge, abrupt, astonishing ones.

There she was in the chair. She had made her choice. That day we sang 'Twinkle, twinkle, little star' together. She moved very quickly after that. Today she belongs to two choirs and has a great, booming laugh. She has been asked to sing in a trio at the next concert.

My greatest desire is that each one of us should have a choice. Know your instrument – this original and sublime instrument with great power to relate in so many ways. Know it all! Make the choice to bellow or be soft, to be slow or fast, to pause or to rush pell-mell with your communication. Choose to be silent, but not to be a slave to silence. Serve the story, serve the song, know who is listening and see how they hear. Above all, listen yourself, for the learning is in the listening. Listen to others, listen to yourself, listen to your environment: it will guide you. And the breathing dragon will become your friend as you reach in and pull out the Grail, filling the cup and drinking from it so that you may fill it again.

It is interesting that I see relatively few performers. Those I work with are actually those who are in trouble. A classical singer might come to me. She is bound into the patriarchal training of her discipline. She will tell me that she is a prisoner of technique, she is being strangled and the joy is gone. We then proceed together to bring the joy back to passionate fire, at the same time acknowledging the necessity for the technique. We look for the middle way where balance is the doorway to renewed creativity and where form and content balance one another. Call it technique and emotional presence if you will.

I think of the voice in two complementarities, the literal and the metaphorical. The literal voice is the instrument itself. Here is a place for bodywork, where together we look for the patterns, those energetic powers within our bodies which keep the full-bodied voice at bay. There is a commonality in the body's response to silence at an early age, even though each story is as unique as a snowflake. From the freedom of the baby in giving sound out of every molecule and cell, the body, so profoundly intelligent, recognises that here is a two-way street. The permeability works in both directions. Impressions are coming into that young vessel even as they are moving out. The body learns to protect its precious holdings, since the impressions from without are too powerful to resist. The muscle structure of the lower belly (which I call the bellows, for it stokes the fire of the breath) begins to contract, creating a kind of armour. This contraction moves upwards and the voice, which travels with the breath as companion and source, moves in the only way possible – up. Women are therefore created to become anti-gravity devices, from high heels and girdles to the sucked-in tummy and the uplifted breasts. We are bombarded with images of the 'perfect look' from such an early age that we can have no resistance. So we suck it in and pull it up and the armour moves ever upward. We arrive at the heart as we arrive at puberty. About this extraordinary event called puberty, I often ask at workshops and seminars 'Did you have a good one?' The reaction is first laughter, then less laughter, then silence – then a collective sigh. Puberty is one of the fundamentals, along with birth and death and several other notable occasions, when the changes in the body and psyche are so profound that we are, as I like to put it, open to the mysteries of the universe. But we are no longer taken by the grandmothers deep into the forest and told the secrets of the family, the history of the tribe. We do not have these necessary rituals, culminating in the joyous acknowledgement that we are women and this is a good and blessed state of being. So we react. The changes happen, our systems are transforming, sexuality is waking up and it feels good. We are told it's bad or we are told nothing. We are told by our peers the misinformation they heard from their older siblings. At this point in history young people are sexually active so early in their lives. The armouring and the silencing become solidified for many at this age. Girls and young women start to live out the fantasy of what they perceive is expected of them, taking in the images that are bombarding them everywhere they look and listen. Their own true voice is subjugated to the glamorous seduction that is everywhere. As adults, we can only be vigilant and compassionate, extending a helping hand to those who ask for it.

The joy of the voice come home is just around the corner. Commitment and practice are required to turn that corner. However, practicality is essential. Can a daily practice consist of an hour's faithful hard work every day? Not on your life! So please, be realistic and discover what will work for you. If it comes down to two minutes a day that is truly available and bearable to work on your voice in whatever way calls to you, begin there. Listen well, both to the inner and the outer voice. When it comes time to seek a guide, be discerning. Look for the place where the courage resides. It is there, as powerful as your heartbeat. There are many ways to work. Will you work with one other? Will you find the right workshop, knowing that a group is your strongest support? Maybe you will join a choir! Find the place that provides the encouragement to keep moving. If not now, when? The story is within, the voice is the teller and it yearns to return home.

Contributors' Notes

Frankie Armstrong was born in Cumbria. She began singing when the skiffle boom hit Britain in 1957 and then became involved in the folk revival. Since 1962 she has built up a repertoire of British songs and ballads which, along with contemporary British songs, still form the basis of her musical vocabulary. The development of her singing style owes much to the influence of AL Lloyd and the traditional women singers of the UK and Ireland. She selects, interprets and writes songs that explore and express personal and social relationships, especially those that focus on the experiences of women.

Frankie suffered severe visual impairment from the age of 17, when she was training for work related to fabric design. She then trained and worked as a social worker, subsequently running workshops on assertiveness training. She combined her social work and passion for singing and voice work up until 1985 when she became a full-time professional singer and voice worker.

Frankie has understood the marginalisation of women performers and is committed to exposing their songs and voices. She was one of several female artists to produce the first ever women-only album in 1966. Frankie has actively worked towards getting women's voices and experiences heard both in song and voice work and has witnessed transformations when women have experienced the power and beauty of their own voices.

As a political activist Frankie performed at public protests against the Vietnam war, for the anti-nuclear movement and on women's issues. Since 1975 she has facilitated Voice Workshops in Britain, Europe, North America and Australia. She has pioneered voice work based on traditional styles of singing, initially influenced by the North American singer and folk song collector Ethel Raim. Her workshops are for singers and non-singers alike, in fact the aim is to do away with this distinction, and they are inspired by cultures where everyone sings as naturally as they talk. The workshops have included participants from a wide range of backgrounds and experience including people of all ages, people from theatre companies, women's groups and special needs groups, and professional performers.

Frankie has appeared on a wide range of recordings along with such performers as AL Lloyd, Ewan MacColl, Peggy Seeger and the Critics Group, Brian Pearson, Roy Bailey and Leon Rosselson. Current solo recordings include the CDs *Ways of Seeing* – acappella with Joan Mills, Venice Manley, Vivien Ellis and a women's choir (Harbourtown); *The Fair Moon Rejoices* – with Joan Mills, Biddy Wells and musicians (Harbourtown); *Till the Grass O'ergrew the Corn* – an album of traditional ballads with Maddy Prior and John Kirkpatrick (Fellside); *Let No One Deceive You: Songs of Bertold Brecht* – with Dave Van Ronk (Flying Fish); *I Heard a Woman Singing* (Flying Fish), *The Garden of Love* (Fellside) and *Lovely on the Water* (Fellside).

Publications:

Armstrong, Frankie, with Kathy Henderson and Sandra Kerr, eds, *My Song is my Own* (a collection of 100 songs about women's lives), Pluto Press, London, 1979

—, with Jenny Pearson, *As Far as the Eye Can Sing* (autobiography), The Women's Press, London, 1992

Chapters contributed to a number of books, the most recent being *Vocal Vision* Marianne Hampton and Barbara Acker, eds, (Applause Books, New York, 1997) and *Ballads into Books: The Legacies of Francis James Child*, Tom Cheeseman and Dsigrid Rienwerts, eds (Peter Lang, Berne, 1997).

Ysaye M Barnwell has performed with the internationally acclaimed acappella quintet, Sweet Honey in the Rock, since 1979. She appears as a vocalist and/or instrumentalist on more than 25 recordings and spends much of her time off-stage as a master teacher and clinician in cultural performance theory and voice production. Her workshop 'Singing in the African-American Tradition' has been conducted all over the United States, Great Britain and Australia. The workshop has been documented in an instructional boxed set of six tapes/CDs with a manual of the same title, produced by Homespun Tapes, Woodstock, NY.

Dr Barnwell has composed and arranged music for many choirs and in a variety of dance, film, video and television projects. In 1996 she won the Bessie Award for her score *Safe House: Still Looking*, commissioned by Liz Lehrman Dance Exchange. As an actress she appeared in the TV series *A Man Called Hawk* and in the film *Beloved*. Her voice can be heard singing on several film sound tracks and she has done voiceover narrations for a number of films and video documentaries. She is author of a children's book, *No Mirrors in My Nana's House* (Harcourt Brace, 1998) and has compiled and edited *Continuum: The First Songbook of Sweet Honey in the Rock*, Sweet Honey in the Rock Contemporary A Capella Press, Maine, 2000.

Daughter of a registered nurse and a violinist, Dr Barnwell studied violin for 15 years. She holds the Batchelor and Masters degrees in speech pathology, a PhD in Craniofacial Studies and a Master of Science in Public Health. She has been a professor at the College of

Dentistry, Howard University, and has implemented health programmes at the Children's Hospital National Medical Center and at Callaudet University, Washington.

Dr Ysaye M Barnwell's Notes, Publishing and Workshop Bookings, 2441 Tunlaw Road, NW Washington, DC 20007-1815, USA.
202-625-1819 (voice)/ 202-6257871 (fax)
e-mail: ymbarnwell.com
web-site: www.ymbarnwell.com

Cicely Berry has been voice director of the Royal Shakespeare Company since she joined in 1969, developing the Company's voice programme so that there is now a three-member voice team working in London and Stratford. From the beginning she has been deeply involved in work in schools, with both teachers and pupils, opening out ways of working with classical text. She has held many weekend sessions for teachers in Stratford and is also involved with work in prisons.

She has worked a great deal with actors and theatre companies abroad, most recently in Brazil, Korea and the United States, where she has an ongoing relationship with Theatre for New Audience in New York, and leads workshops with theatre directors. She has worked in many European countries as well as Australia, India, China, Zimbabwe, Bulgaria, Croatia and Russia. In 1997 she organised a seminar on 'Theatre and Development' and a debate on 'Theatre and Citizenship' at the Barbican Theatre, two highly successful events with representatives from leading aid organisations as well as theatre companies from many countries.

She has directed productions of *Hamlet* for the National Theatre Education Unit and *King Lear* for the RSC. She and Andrew Wade directed two multicultural programmes of prose and poetry with RSC actors, *Words, Words, Words* in 1994–95 and *More Words* in 1997. In 1985 she was awarded the OBE and in 1992 was nominated for an award by the Arts Council for 'her response to the challenges posed by a technologically diverse and increasingly multicultural environment'. She received an Honorary Doctorate of Letters from Birmingham University in 1999.

Publications:
See Bibliography p53.

Roz Comins is co-ordinator and founder of the Voice Care Network UK, a unique group of voice teacher/coaches and specialist speech and language therapists. She is one of 100 UK tutors who provide highly focused Voice Workshops in schools, colleges and Teacher Centres. Roz trained as a teacher at Central School of Speech and Drama, taught in London Education Authority and independent schools, brought up a family and was a lecturer at Coventry Technical College. She provided voice work, directed plays with theatre students and operas with the School of Music, toured 'Literary Takeaway' programmes, introduced presentation skills for managers and assisted in English Speaking Board Examinations. She was a member of the working party that founded the Voice Research Society (which merged with the British Voice Association). All this experience helped to create the Voice Care Network and supported her revision of its booklet *More Care For Your Voice*, an extended version of the original booklet *Care For Your Voice*, which sold several thousand copies over the seven years it was in circulation.
Publications:
More Care For Your Voice, compiled by VCN members and edited by Yvonne Morley, Caroline Cornish, Shirley Crawford, Roz and David Comins, published by Voice Care Network UK, Kenilworth, 1999

Articles:
Comins, Roz, 'Voice tuition for professional voice users: a

tutor's account', *Voice: Journal of the BVA*, 4, Vol 1, (1995)
—'Helping people to keep their voices healthy and to communicate effectively', *Journal of Language and Communication Disorders*, Vol 33, Supplement (1998)
—'Voice Care', *Croner Teachers' Briefing*, 67; 71 (1999)

Favourite books:
Crystal, David, *The Cambridge Encyclopedia of Language*, Cambridge University Press, Cambridge, 1987
Berry, Cicely, *Your Voice and How to Use It*, Harrap, London, 1975; revised Virgin, London, 1994
Dunbar, Robin, *Grooming Gossip and the Evolution of Language*, Faber and Faber, London, 1996

Olivea Dewhurst-Maddock was born in Surrey in 1934 and grew up in Farnsworth (now part of Greater Manchester), the adopted daughter of a portrait photographer and a horticulturalist/florist, both of whom were music lovers. She started to sing when three years old, was privately educated, and trained in the Italian tradition of Manuel Garcia (ARCM). She joined Sadlers Wells Opera as a singer in 1962. She became interested in therapy by watching the effect of music on people and acquired training in meditation and complementary techniques. She sang for Sir George Trevelyan and the Wrekin Trust, The Prometheus School, Hygeia College, Hawkwood College and The Oracle School of Colour. Her book *Healing With Sound* was published in 1993 and she has contributed to other publications on the subject of music therapy.

Olivea has been involved in adult education for many years and has worked for the Workers Education Association, and in further education. She is voice tutor to Poulton-le-Fylde College of Education; offers workshops and courses from home; and she directs and produces for opera and music 'theatre groups'. Her interests include inter-faith spirituality, wildlife and animal welfare, painting and needlework, gardening and enjoying the lakeland countryside around her home. She is married to Jack Dewhurst-Maddock, a retired cricket professional and former farmer.

Publications:
See Bibliography p191.

Michele George is a voice specialist who has been working professionally and therapeutically with voice for 20 years. Born in Canada, she has acted, sung and directed on four continents and is a founder member of Peter Brook's International Centre for Theatre Research, in which she spent 10 years as an actor. She holds a diploma from the Central School of Speech and Drama in London, a Bachelor of Arts degree in Speech and Dramatic Arts and the *Freddie Stone Memorial Award in Music*, which is presented annually in Canada for a musician of integrity and innovation. She continues to perform, especially singing, from 'the fearless place for which she is eternally grateful'. She is also a popular speaker and seminar leader at human potential conferences in North America and Europe.

Michele was analysed by Marion Woodman, the Jungian analyst, with whom she leads mind/body workshops through the CG Jung Foundation in Toronto. She works as a therapist in private practice, offering personally crafted sessions of vocal exploration and re-membering, which she calls Re:Sound. She works with individual clients and groups to 'discover the natural voice within each one of us and welcome it as the communicator, singer and storyteller it was always meant to be'. Her practice is in Toronto, but she travels far and wide to work with both women and men, spreading her inspirational message of the possibility of bringing the voice back home again and claiming the birthright which was silenced. She also works as a corporate consultant, helping people to bring presentation skills to a high level in corporate culture. Her popular tapes *Drink from the Well* and *River of Song* are available through 'Sounds True' in Colorado (1-800-333-9185).

Jenny Goodman has sung all her life and has been working with voice and song, mostly in community settings, since 1990. She trained with Frankie Armstrong and is strongly influenced by Frankie's approach. She combines her voice work skills with her skills in community work: she holds a Postgraduate Certificate in Community Education from Moray House College of Education in Edinburgh. In 1992 she established the Voice House in Edinburgh – a 'community which sings' of over 100 members – and she is still its musical director. Since writing her chapter for this book she has returned to full time employment as a voice and song specialist and has been awarded a place on Central School of Speech and Drama's MA in Voice Studies.

Three books which have influenced Jenny's approach to voice and song are Kristin Linklater's *Freeing the Natural Voice*, Patsy Rodenburg's *The Right to Speak* and Ysaye Barnwell's *Continuum: The First Song Book of Sweet Honey in the Rock*.

Kristin Linklater is chair of the Graduate Theatre Division of the School of Arts at Columbia University, New York City, where she teaches voice, text and Shakespeare. She was born and brought up in Scotland and trained as an actor at the London Academy of Music and Dramatic Art, where she subsequently returned to teach voice production as Iris Warren's assistant. She moved to the United States in 1963 and she taught voice production to actors in theatre trainings and regional theatre companies throughout the United States and abroad. From 1966 to 1978 she was on the faculty of the New York University Graduate Theatre

Program and coached theatre companies including the Festival Theatre at Stratford, Ontario, the Lincoln Centre Repertory Company and the Royal Shakespeare Company as well as Broadway shows, including the original production of *Hair*. She received several prestigious grants to support The Working Theatre, NY, her programme for training teachers of voice, movement and acting (1974–79), and in 1983 she was awarded a Guggenheim Fellowship for the development of Shakespeare actor-training methods. She was co-founder with Tina Packer of Shakespeare and Company at The Mount, Lennox, MA, and served as its Director of Training for 12 years. From 1990–97 she was Director of Training at Emerson College, Boston and co-director with Carol Gilligan of The Company of Women, an all-female Shakespeare company dedicated to strengthening the voices of women and girls. During these years she also acted and directed. She has played Shakespearean and contemporary roles and given one-woman shows and poetry readings.

Publications:
Linklater, Kristin, *Freeing the Natural Voice*, Drama Book Publishers, New York, 1976
—*Freeing Shakespeare's Voice: The Actor's Guide to Talking the Text*, Theatre Communications Group, New York, 1992

Julie McNamara is second generation Irish. Her father was Catholic and her mother Protestant. One might suppose then that conflict intervention is a skill she was raised with. She often credits her home life with providing the impetus for her work in trouble spots around the globe. She is a campaigner in the field of mental health and works as co-ordinator of London Disability Arts Festivals. She is also a trainer and drama therapist, running workshops in a variety of arts establishments. She is renowned for her singing and song writing which earned her a Vinyl Dreams award through the Arts Council in January 1999. She has taught voice workshops throughout Europe and the Caribbean for over a decade. The main thrust of her work is directed towards groups of people who are often overlooked in the mainstream arts world or whose access is limited. In June 1999 she was awarded a Movers and Shapers award from East Midlands Shape for her outstanding contribution to equality of access in the arts. She is one of a rare breed in her commitment to creating change. Her concerts and workshops are a unique experience, a challenge to conventional thinking and a celebration of difference.

Publications:
See Bibliography p95.

Joan Mills is a highly experienced voice teacher, theatre director and singer who has taught voice and singing work-shops in a wide variety of contexts, for professional perform-ers and theatre companies as well as the community at large. Following four successful years as Director of the Young People's Theatre Scheme at the Royal Court, she became Director of Theatre Powys in mid-Wales and then worked freelance. She was for eight years a lecturer in Vocal Studies at the Welsh College of Music and Drama, including three years as Head of Music and Movement. She has directed and lectured at a variety of other institutions including Dartington College of Art, the Universities of Aberystwyth and Leicester, and the Central School of Speech and Drama.

Joan's approach to voice work is playful and accessible but allows real changes to occur. She works with the participants to free the body and therefore the voice from unnecessary tension by encouraging total body/breath/ voice co-ordination. Her work incorporates principles from Tai Chi and the Alexander Technique as well as the major theatre-voice practices and is influenced by her own studies with eminent vocal practitioners from around the world and the UK.

She regularly performs as a singer herself, particularly alongside her colleague and friend Frankie Armstrong. They can be heard together on the CDs *Ways of Seeing* and *The Fair Moon Rejoices* (Harbourtown). In 1995 she sang and toured in *The Soundhouse*, a performance created by Meredith Monk in collaboration with the Centre for Performance Research.

Joan is the Director of Giving Voice, a project of CPR which celebrates and explores the voice in performance by bringing voice practitioners from around the world to work within the context of a specific theme. She is currently preparing a book, *A Divinity of the Voice*, and working on a source book of the voice for Methuen. A book by which she has been greatly influenced over the years is Rollo May's *The Courage to Create*.

Vayu Naidu is a storyteller, performer and writer. She was awarded Europe's first PhD in Indian performance oral traditions at the University of Leeds (1994). She has toured internationally, performing at storytelling, literature and music festivals, and was Visiting Lecturer at the Department of Drama and Theatre Arts, University of Birmingham, from 1995–98. She is the founder and artistic director of Brumhalta Intercultural Storytelling Company, based in Birmingham, and she performs solo, accompanied by music, with the Vayu Naidu: Ka Tha Company. She has worked in storytelling performance alongside Ustad Zakir Hussain, Pandit Shiv Kumar Sharma and a number of British contemporary music composers.

In 1999 Vayu won the BBC Radio Drama *Chasing the Rainbow* playwriting competition with her play *There comes a Karma*, which was broadcast in November 1999. Her play *Krishna's Lila: Playboy of the Asian world* was produced at the Leicester Haymarket Theatre. Here, too, she wrote and performed *Ramayana*, directed by Chris Banfield. She is currently Artistic Associate of NATAK (Asian Theatre Initiative) at the Leicester Haymarket Theatre, a post in which she commissions new writing from Asians in Britain, and writing in English from the subcontinent for production at the studio and main house. In 1998 she was Writer in Residence at Bishop Grosseteste College, Lincoln, funded by the Arts Council, and produced an anthology, *Writing from the Wall*, which includes work she did with inmates of Lincoln Prison.

Publications:
Naidu, Vayu, *Eyes on the Peacock's Tail; A Curly Tale; Hiss! Don't Bite; and The Magic Vessels*, Tulka, Chennai, 1998, (a retelling of four Indian folk tales, available on audio, published by Sky).
—*Stories from India*, Hodder Wayland, London, 1999

Annie Neligan, a member of the National Women's Self-Defence Teachers Association, started teaching self-defence to women 16 years ago. Until then she had been teaching geography to usually reluctant schoolchildren. She loved the change to working with women, bringing them skills they really wanted at a time in their lives when they knew why they wanted them. And she enjoyed putting into practice her commitment to widening women's opportunities and choices in a practical and positive way. Since then she has worked mostly in community education with women from different communities in Sheffield and Yorkshire. With others she has developed opportunities for training as teachers of self-defence, in this region and more recently in Lithuania and Russia. Her practice has grown as part of a network of self-defence teachers sharing their ideas, skills and experience. In particular, Helen Lyle has encouraged and enabled her to find power in her voice.

She has become increasingly interested in supporting women to build their physical confidence and increase their sense of personal power in the face not just of violence but of all sorts of intimidation and prejudice. To this she brings perspectives shaped by years of involvement in anti-racist, internationalist and socialist movements. She believes that to have autonomy and choice we need to change not only ourselves but, most of all, the systems which imprison us all!

Favourite books on self-defence:
Quinn, Khaleghi, *Stand Your Ground*, Channel 4, London, 1992
Wiley, Carol A, ed, *Women in the Martial Arts*, North Atlantic Books, Berkeley, California, 1992

Jenny Pearson has been writing and publishing since the age of nine, read English at Bristol University, trained on *The Times* and worked there as a reporter and feature writer. She then freelanced for the national press, producing occasional non-fiction books. She became active in storytelling in the mid-eighties, starting the Kew Storytellers, and subsequently the Brentford Storytellers – a weekly storytelling workshop at Watermans Arts Centre. Here she hosted performance evenings, giving a platform to a new generation of professional storytellers as well as some of the great tellers of the Traveller tradition. The format of the Watermans evenings, with stories told from the floor and a visiting performer, moved with Jenny to North London in 1989, when she started the 'Camden Storytellers Ceilidh' at the Torriano Meeting House in Kentish Town, envisaged as a 'ceilidh house' where people gather to entertain one another with stories and music. This is still flourishing after 11 years. Jenny runs workshops and courses in storytelling and in 1995 she created the Bleddfa Week of Storytelling which takes place every August in mid-Wales.

Her fascination with traditional stories and the profound

effect they can have on people led Jenny to train in 1989–90 as a drama and movement therapist on the Jungian-based Sesame course at Central School of Speech and Drama. She has practised drama and movement therapy with emotionally disturbed children and other groups. After training she researched and edited the first book about Sesame. She is a member of the Sesame staff team at Central, has done further training as a psychodynamic counsellor and psychotherapist and has a private practice in North London.

Publications:

Armstrong, Frankie and Jenny Pearson, *As Far As The Eye Can Sing*, The Women's Press, London, 1992

Lambert, Jack and Jenny Pearson, with *Adventure Playgrounds*, Jonathan Cape and Penguin, London, 1974

Pearson, Jenny, ed, *Discovering the Self Through Drama and Movement: The Sesame Approach*, Jessica Kingsley, London, 1996

—assisted in the writing of Dame Diana Rigg's *No Turn Unstoned*, Elm Tree Books, London, 1982

—*Composing Myself*, (autobiography of Sir Andrzej Panufnik), Methuen, London, 1987

Inspired by:

Sawyer, Ruth, *The Way of the Storyteller*, Bodley Head, London, 1942

van der Post, Laurens, *The Heart of the Hunter*, Penguin, London, 1967

Williamson, Duncan, *A Thorn in the King's Foot, Stories of the Scottish Travelling People*, Penguin, London, 1987

Noírín Ní Riain, an internationally renowned spiritual singer, was born in Caherconlish, Co. Limerick in 1951. She studied music at University College, Cork, graduating with a Masters degree in traditional religious song in Irish in 1980. Her vast CD repertory includes a trilogy of recordings with the Benedictine monks of Glenstal Abbey – *Caoineadh na Malghdine, Good People All, Vox de Nube* – several solos, notably *Stor Amhran, Soundings, Celtic Soul*. She is the author of three books, the most recent being *Gregorian Chant Experience* (book and CD, The O'Brien Press).

Noírín has shared performances with Gregory Peck, Anjelica Huston, Sinead O'Connor, John Cage, His Holiness XIV Dalai Lama and sung at four United Nations conferences world-wide.

She is currently Artist-in-Residence in Co. Laois – the first ever singer to be appointed to such an Arts position in Ireland. She is also pursuing doctoral studies in Theology. The scope and novelty of her dissertation will be to define the power of sound to elicit and create religious experience. Such transformative sound she labels THEOSONY, which is her own portmanteau word deriving from 'theology' and 'sonance'.

Patsy Rodenburg is head of the Voice Department at the Royal National Theatre and the Guildhall School of Music and Drama. She trained at the Central School of Speech and Drama. She has taught and presented workshops internationally in North America, Australia, Japan, India, and throughout Europe. She is an Associate of the Michael Howard Studios, New York, and an Associate of the Royal Court Theatre. She has worked with the Royal Shakespeare Company, English Shakespeare Company, Cheek-by-Jowl, Donmar, Theatre de Complicite, Almeida, Shared Experience Theatre, the National Theatre of Greece and Tokyo's Grand Kabuki Company. She has been a Distinguished Visiting Professor at the Meadows School of the Arts, Southern Methodist University in Dallas, Texas, and organised the voice programme at the Stratford Festival Theatre in Stratford, Canada.

In addition to her work with actors, Patsy has taught countless people in other walks of life to realise the full potential of their voices. Through her own organisation, The Voice and Speech Centre, she offers voice and speech consultation and seminars to performing artists, film companies, advertising and media specialists, business executives, education groups and therapists. Her work has also taken her into inner city schools, prisons and various rehabilitation institutions. She has published three books and, recently, a video in which she demonstrates methods developed over 20 years of teaching voice production, showing that it is within the reach of everyone to improve the voice and speak with confidence. The video carries an explicit 'Exemption' from the usual restrictions, stating on the cover that 'Permission is granted by the copyright owners for the video to be used indefinitely for educational purposes'.

Publications:
Rodenburg, Patsy, *The Right to Speak*, Methuen, London, 1992
—*The Need for Words*, Methuen, London, 1993
—*The Actor Speaks*, Methuen, London, 1996

Video:
A Voice of Your Own: How to Speak so that People will Want to Listen, Vanguard Productions, PO Box 70, Norwich NR1 2ED